IN AFRICA

EVEN THE FLIES ARE HAPPY

IN AFRICA
EVEN THE FLIES
ARE HAPPY

SELECTED POEMS 1964–1977

Breyten Breytenbach

translated by Denis Hirson

JOHN CALDER

LONDON

In Africa Even The Flies Are Happy first published in Great Britain in 1978 by
John Calder (Publishers) Ltd.,
18 Brewer Street, London W1R 4AS
Copyright © 1976, 1977 by Yolande Breytenbach and Meulenhoff Nederland,
    Amsterdam
These translations © John Calder (Publishers) Ltd.

Typeset in Theme 10pt by The Pentagon Printing Group, London
Printed by M & A Thomson Litho Ltd., East Kilbride
Bound by Hunter & Foulis Ltd., Edinburgh

CONTENTS

POETRY

Die Ysterkoei Moet Sweet
(The Iron Cow Must Sweat) 1964

Die Huis van die Dowe
(The House of the Deaf) 1967

v

'n Seisoen in die Paradys *(A Season in Paradise)* 1976

Prison Poems 1975 — 1977

Other poems

PROSE

TRANSLATOR'S FOREWORD

As work on these translations progressed, I found my approach changing. In particular, there was a tendency in my earlier drafts to be lyrical and soft, and to make obvious grammatical sense, when this was not always reflected in the original texts. Breyten Breytenbach's Afrikaans is particularly chopped and changed, the syntax often broken, nouns newly compacted. I hope that the translations as they now stand go further in revealing such elements.

Among those people who helped with the translations, I would like in particular to mention: Robert Berold; Ampie Coetzee; Jean de Bay; Baruch Hirson; Yael Hirson; Georges Lory; Kelwyn Sole and Adriaan van Dis. And a special thanks to Fredrick van der Vyver with whose assistance many of these words were goaded into the night.

D.H.
1978

PRINCIPLE DATES

16.9.1939   Born in Bonnievale, Cape Province.

Studied for B.A. at the University of Cape Town.

1959   Left South Africa by freighter for Europe; worked in a factory in England, as a cook on a private yacht off Nice, etc.

1961   Settled in Paris, engaged in painting, writing poems and stories. Married Ngo Thi Hoang Lien Yolande.

1962   First exhibition of paintings at the Edinburgh Paperback Gallery.

1964   Publication of a first book of poems, *Die ysterkoei moet sweet;* also, a book of short stories, *Katastrofes.* Together, they were awarded the Afrikaanse Pers Beperk (Afrikaans Press Corporation) prize.

Exhibitions at Galerie Girardon, Paris; Galerie Espace, Amsterdam; Galerie 20, Arnhem. Participation in group exhibitions at Galerie Legendre, Galerie Lahumiere and Galerie Claude Levin, all in Paris.

1965   Exhibitions at Galerie Contour, Bruxelles; Galerie Waalkens, Groningue. Participation in group exhibitions at Gallery 12, Minneapolis; Salon de la jeune peinture, Paris; Biennale de Paris; Galerie Peintres du Monde and Galerie le soleil dans la tête, both in Paris.

1966   Exhibitions at Galerie Claude Levin and Galerie Tournesol, Paris; Galerie Espace, Amsterdam. Participation in group exhibitions at Salon de la jeune peinture; Galerie la Roue, Rotterdam; Galerie Delta, Paris.

1967   A second book of peoms, *Huis van die dowe* published, and awarded the South African Central News Agency prize.

1969   Similarly, *Kouevuur* (poems) awarded the South African Central News Agency prize.

1970   *Lotus* (poems). Yet another South African News Agency prize. Also, *Oorblyfsels* (poems).

1971   *Om te vlieg* (story). Exhibition of paintings at Rotterdam Arts Foundation, Rotterdam.

1972   *Skryt* (poems). Awarded the Dutch Van der Hoogt prize. Exhibition at Galerie Espace, Amsterdam.

1973   Publication of *Met ander woorde* (poems). Granted a three-month visa to visit South Africa with his wife, despite her classification as 'non-white'. Made a speech at an Afrikaans writers' conference in Cape Town, telling participants that their people were doomed to destruction through self-isolation, and appealing to them to do something about it.

1974   Exhibition at Galerie Espace, Amsterdam.

1975   Entered South Africa in disguise, armed with a false passport. Arrested three months later, in November, and charged under the Terrorism Act with being instrumental in the formation of Okhela (Zulu for 'spark'), a white wing of the African National Congress. The aim of the organisation was allegedly to bring about revolutionary change in South Africa under leadership of the black liberation movement by various means, including armed struggle. He pleaded guilty, was sentenced to nine years imprisonment.

1976   Publication of *Voetskrif* (poems). Awarded a prize by the Perskor newspaper group. Exhibition at Galerie Espace, Amsterdam. Publication of *'n Seisoen in die paradys* (recounting the 1973 journey).

1977   Exhibitions: La Dérive, Paris; Rotterdam Arts Foundation, Rotterdam.

April: International Publisher's Prize *(Prix des Septs)* given to German poet Erich Fried; Breytenbach given a special award, in terms of which he will be translated into Spanish, Portuguese, German, further translated into French, Dutch. This book contains the English translation.

June: Still in prison, after 1½ years in solitary confinement next to the death cell, Breytenbach put on trial again. Charged under Terrorism, Riotous Assemblies and Prisons Act with trying to escape, promoting an underground movement to fight apartheid while in prison, and smuggling out letters, poems. Acquitted of all but the last charge, for which he was fined.

from

Die Yysterkoei Moet Sweet

(The Iron Cow must Sweat)

1964

Bedreiging van die Siekes

(vir B. Breytenbach)

Dames en Here, vergun my om u voor te stel aan Breyten
            Breytenbach,
die maer man met die groen trui; hy is vroom
en stut en hamer sy langwerpige kop om vir u
'n gedig te fabriseer   soos byvoorbeeld:
ek is bang om my oë toe te maak
ek wil nie in die donker leef *en* sien wat aangaan nie
die hospitale van Parys is stampvol bleek mense
wat voor die vensters staan en dreigend beduie
soos die engele in die oond
dit reën die strate afgeslag en glyerig

my oë is gestysel
hulle/julle sal my op so 'n nat dag begrawe
as die sooie rou swart vleis is
en die blare en oorryp blomme gekleur en geknak is van nat
voordat die lig hulle kan knaag,   die lug sweet wit bloed
maar ek sal weier om my oë in te hok

pluk my benerige vlerke af
die mond is té geheim om pyn nie te voel nie
trek stewels aan vir my begrafnis sodat ek die modder
aan julle voete kan hoor soen
die spreeus kantel hul gladde lekkende koppe, swart bloeisels
die groen bome is prewelende monnike

plant my op 'n heuwel naby 'n dam onder leeubekkies
laat die sluwe bitter eende op my graf kak
in die reën
die siele van kranksinnige maar geslepe vrouens vaar in katte in
vrese vrese vrese met deurweekte kleurlose koppe
en ek sal weier om my swart tong te troos (kalmeer)

Kyk hy is skadeloos, wees hom tog genadig.

Threat of the Sick

(for B. Breytenbach)

Ladies and Gentlemen, allow me to introduce you to Breyten
            Breytenbach,
the lean man in the green sweater; he is devout
and braces and hammers his oblong head
to fabricate a poem for you   for example:
I am scared to close my eyes
I don't want to live in the dark *and* see what goes on
the hospitals of Paris are crammed with pasty people
standing at the windows making threatening gestures
like the angels in the furnace
it's raining the streets flayed and slippery

my eyes are starched
on a wet day like this they/you will bury me
when the sods are raw black flesh
the leaves and jaded flowers snapped and stained with wetness
before the light can gnaw at them,   the sky sweats white blood
but I will refuse to coop up my eyes

pluck my bony wings
the mouth is too secretive not to feel pain
wear boots to my funeral so I can hear the mud
kissing your feet
like black blossoms the starlings tilt their smooth leaking heads
the green trees are monks, muttering

plant me on a hill near a pool under snapdragons
let the furtive bitter ducks crap on my grave
in the rain
cats are possessed by the souls of crazed yet cunning women
fears fears fears with drenched colourless heads
and I will refuse to comfort (soothe) my black tongue

Look he is harmless, have mercy on him

Death sets in at the feet

One should simply drift off
(but they say that for 48 hours at least the consciousness
waits at the steamed-up windows of the skull beating
      like a fish in a basket
      or a space traveller in a spacetube beyond control
      of a jew under a pyramid of jews
      or a nigger(lover) in a cell)
with a prickling of pins that begins in the soles.

But is that what it's like?
This giddiness as the floor tilts
and a membrane of water draws over the trees
and a zealous hand clutches the throat more tightly.
And what a farce, this fumbling for images.

Last week's chrysanthemums are already rotten
on their stems the green veins now perished rubber pipes;
The one-time yapping parrots
are now limp and shrivelled wigs.

The day before yesterday's white carnations stink,
slumped old women.
Yesterday's red roses already have a deeper bloom,
disjointed fists.

People usually die flat on their backs
feet cold and erect as petrified rabbits
or blossoms on a branch
with a prickling of pins that begins in the soles.

My feet are hostile towards me I must appease them
swaddle them in cloth, because I am not yet ready
because I must still learn how to die
because I must still decide how to go about it

Because now I gaze through a mirror into a riddle
but tommorrow it will be face to face

Write off

why should the arabs come to my window
at night when only the clocks are alive
droning their miserable tunes
full of need and nostalgia

I must also go to bed and wait
for the rats of my feet to stifle
and grow still under the blankets. I also
like stroking an Africa of green

clay in the chart of my brain.
Go spew out your gruesome bat-like emotions
somewhere else: the chambers of
my head are all occupied

breyten prays for himself

There is no need for Pain Lord[2]
We could live well enough without It
A flower has no teeth

It is true we are only fulfilled in death
But let our flesh stay new as fresh cabbage
Make us firm as a fish's pink body
Let us spellbind each other with eyes deep butterflies

Pardon our mouths our guts our brains
Let us regularly taste the sweet evening air
Swim in tepid seas, be allowed to sleep with the sun
Ride peacefully on bicycles through bright Sundays

And gradually we will rot like old ships or trees
But keep Pain far from Me o Lord
That others may bear it
Be taken into custody, Shattered
                        Stoned
                        Hanged
                        Lashed
                        Used
                        Tortured
                        Crucified
                        Interrogated
                        Placed under house arrest
                        Made to slave their guts out

Banished to obscure islands till the end of their days
Wasting in damp pits down to slimy green imploring bones
Worms in their stomachs heads full of nails
But not *Me*
Never give us Pain or complain

hiiiiieeeeeeee

these sweet potato runners alongside the railroad
just how painful
their ears must be

blind a

now that it's so still that you'll
be able to hear them scream, the tattered
snow the countless colourless bats

the houses thicken an entire city
rises like raw bread now that it's so still
that you'll be able to hear them scream

the bloodless bits of flesh sticking
to the panes those are gods shot
through belly and buttock, with a futile battle

tomorrow the trees will be bearded with age
I'd have liked to ride a bicycle through the park
a thin flea crossing the heavens of the white woman

flowers for buddha

(I) breathe in (I) breathe
out (I) breathe an abundance
in
  and
out
and smell moons of mimosa in tiny bunches
yellow as summer

and the hushed hush
at your forehead
as in summer at noon

(I) breathe a summer a hush
and the scent of tiny bunched moons of mimosa
an abundance
in
  and
out
  and
in

co la

the heron wheels desolate in the wind
the sun is warm as a goat's udder
I walk across the bridge
with my shivering face in the water
do you still think of me sometimes?
I see you at home in the garden behind my eyes
your white teeth shining in the sun
my sheet is wet with dreams

the heron screams for his mate across the lupins
the sky sloughs off teeth snow silence
crust over the town I stand on the bridge
with my disfigured self flat on the water
do you still think of me sometimes?
you turn in my head like a sombre tune
your white hands playing in the sun
my sheet is piping with dreams

guide to the seasons[3]

kissing you leads me to think
of vineyards   gaunt in the sodden winters
green as the moon in summer   and in autumn
the amber and the blue
and the rustling rain
of
falling
leaves

the amber and the blue
when the earth is fragrant   and I (kiss)[3] you

so it's true you hide the 4 seasons in your cheeks

from

Die Huis van die Dowe

(The House of the Deaf)

1967

Fiësta vir 'n oog

om dan die koors uit die liggaam te laat
soos wind die seile verlaat
of 'n vuis oopbreek om die gekluisde vlieg te bevry

jy ken geen ander vyeboom wat so staan
so oopgekloof staan deur die beul van son
staan en bloei oor sy werpsel koelte
en sy vye vol verhemeltes stop om die son te kan tart later
geen boom is so die moeder van koelte
waarin huwelike voltrek word nie
waar die stewige stam ingepas word
in die mondrooi mond van die grond
vlees wek vlees
en die vye is vol melk

jy ken geen ander plaat turksvye
met die blaaie vol rooi en sappige vratte
waar die ou vrouens so donker soos mispels
so donker soos verniste kerkies in hulle swart rokke
die bokke kom melk

jy ken geen ander wysgere soos die grys olyfboom
met 'n staf gestut onder elke tak
met sy bladsye wat prewel van wind

jy ken green ander wit huise wat agter klipmure tril
as die boomsingertjies sing
die trotse gebalsemde harte
waaruit die bloedliggame kom die ou vrouens
wat die bokke kom melk
by die turksvye

jy ken geen ander kreupeldenne met sulke wit maskers
jou oog sien geen wolk behalwe dié wat op die see dryf
en geen ander akkedis as die klein groen gids
die geitjie met sy wegwysterstert na die son

geen sterre wat so oor die harte kom pluk
om die vrouens uit te lok
sodat hulle die bokke kan melk
by die turksvye

14

Fiesta for an eye

then to release the fever from the body
like wind quitting the sails
or a fist breaking open to free the trapped fly

you know no other fig tree which stands
as this one stands cleaved by the butchering sun
bleeding over its litter of coolness
stuffing its figs full of palates so that later it can taunt the sun
no tree rivals this mother of coolness
where wedlock is celebrated
where the firm root is fitted
to the red-mouthed orifice in the ground
flesh rouses flesh
and the figs are full of milk

you know no other patch of prickly pears
leaves covered with juicy red warts
where the old women dark as medlars
dark as lacquered small churches in their black skirts
come to milk the goats

you know no other philosophers like this grey olive tree
with a staff propped under every branch
with its pages muttering in the wind

you know no other white houses trembling behind stone walls
when the cicadas sing
blood-cells emerge
from the proud embalmed hearts, old women
to milk the goats
near the prickly pears

you know no other crippled pines bearing masks so white
your eye picks out only that cloud floating on the sea
and no lizard but this small green guide
the gecko, its tail pointing the ways to the sun

no stars which cross hearts, plucking at them like this
tempting the women out
to milk the goats
near the prickly pears

en geen see geen amandel geen rustige oog
en geen rus of berusting of kelders of die koelte van slaap

in die ooste kom 'n nuwe rooi koors soos 'n saad in 'n skedel
'n laatson-seilboot uitgeswel in die wind
'n vlieg sonder vlerke in 'n bloederige vuis
'n oog wat die feesmaal kom wy

(7/8/66 — Formentera)

and no sea no almond tree no restful eye
and no rest or surrender or cellars or the cool of sleep

from the east a fresh red fever approaches like a seed in a skull
a sailboat against the low sun puffed out in the wind
a fly without wings in a blood-covered fist
an eye come to consecrate the feast

(7/8/66 — Formentera)

Fly-tamer on Espalmador

From apple-red day onwards I labour like a king
to crush flies in my palms —
in the evening when the moon fires her small silver pistols
black little thoughts come to harass me
under the gold palm tree

The moon's hair is filled with damp smoke
the palm tree folds its fingers towards the light —
and since there's no burial-place for the flies
their buzzing still torments me —
tomorrow the apples will also explode

Landscape with dead sheep

First the commonplace:
summer's back is already broken —
he drags his bones slowly to the sea,
by day the sky bluer, deeper,
grey and black autumn blossoms/crape
cakes the branches
and smells the grave in each of use, disclosing it,
the southbound 'planes are full of swallows and storks,
and as the world grows vague around us
our breaths put on shirts again

And now for the exceptions:
O Diviner of the Stars,
is there no deliverance or chance
of escape?
Will we ever again
sleep under palm trees?
And why does everything smell
so tender, so fragrant?
For the last time?
A dead sheep passes the door

And the earth is nibbled bright,
nothing for our breaths to graze —
we chat old corpses in Sunday best

Like slaked lime

my fire is slaked
I must stand to one side
it's rain that strikes against the roof
and tears the heart from its pulsing water sac
the ear withdraws itself from sound dripping

what I could not feel in my heart
I could not establish in my head
what do I know of my land and its problems
what when its trees scorch
(how furious I could be)
I don't trust in its future
and know that its past decomposes in stench
each day I remember less of its language
it's rain that strikes against the roof

rain is conversion
and rain is knowledge
and rain is the abhorrent blunting of vowels
and rain is nerve-fibres bound rain is sinkers

I know nothing now of mountain or wind
hear too little to sing along
in the choir
besides the heart has lost its peels and pride
it's rain that strikes against the roof

I neither am nor am not
gentlemen I stand at your disposal stripped
for the highest bidder
for whoever can keep the rain from my ears
and show me how cunningly a man's fingers can conjure

it's rain that stands over the skies
I have no more fight my fire is doused
it's rain that gives life to new leaves
the most repulsive ears on trees
nails on a corpse

all things swell closed:
drought sets in as well, and yet
in the stillness of the inner ear
you can now be coupled with a self —
your small deaf self listening within the ear

The open sky (with torelli inside)

I stand crying in the blue rain
under the enchanted tree

blotches of music break out incessantly
in small blue leaves across me

the tree like a flower a bride tousled
under birds showering music

until I'm as clean as dreamy as blue
washed here and there by my tree
full of needles full of yearning

sing sing my tree pouring birds
sing whispering green fog over me
sing sweet hands onto my neck

I stand further within the blue lounge and gaze
and gaze at the blue dissolving self
glistening so blessed

(from) *Ars Poetica*

Traveller from Hell-and-Gone
where the grapes hang blue with milk
and the mouse-birds blow out fresh blossoms

Tell me of my people
Speak, break open your bitter breath
Let your talk fill my night with Southern Crosses

*

a respectable cat
worth its scales
ought
to hatch an egg
within 24 hours

*

my
arsehole is full of
myself

*

(pretty lizurd)

just as the lizard is related
            to the bunch of green grapes
so the crocodile is akin to the cypress
and the word decides the thought

*

23

(the wandering afrikaner)

my poems go no further than a day trip
and I'm a globe-trotter
from day to day
from hand to mouth
as thirsty as ever
and less inquisitive
searching non-stop for another old star

meanwhile my poems are just day trips

from

Kouevuur

(**Gangrene;** literally, Cold fire)

1969

Tiberius se grot digby Sperlonga in Latium

Tiberius — Romein en Keiser
het hier, omring deur fraai kunswerke
sy somervakansies op sy jis gesit
in sale uit die berg gekap

Hier is daar gefuif, gerinkink,
is meer as een transaksie beklink
terwyl buite Romeine, Onderdane
in die middaghitte sit en stink
klein en bruin soos drolle

Sy gekerkerde oog kon seer sekerlik wei
oor 'n geordende wêreld —
oor mure en dyke in die water
waaragter vis en reptiel geteel
vir die verhemelte of bloot
vir vermaak
opslaggies maak,
en verder, hoe oor die glasgroen weiland
sý bote op lang spane loop

Sodat hy aandliks — wanneer die rooi god
agter die kaap 'n rooi toga in die branders laat —
in geselskap en pretensie van vetgat-senatore
welgeluksalig die volumes van sy blanke liggaam
in die staande varswater van sy marmerswembad kon waad

Tiberius' cave near Sperlonga in Latium

Tiberius — a Roman and a Caesar
sat here all on his own during his summer holidays
ringed by elegant works of art
in halls hewn from the mountain

Which saw banquets, debauchery,
and the clinching of more than one deal
while outside Romans and Subjects
sat in the mid-day heat small and brown
stinking like turds

His imprisoned eye could no doubt wander
across a well-ordered world —
across walls and dykes in the water
behind which fish and reptiles were bred
for the palate
or exhibited
simply for entertainment,
and beyond that, how his own galleys stalked
over glassgreen meadows on long oars

So that in the evening — when the red god
behind the cape trailed a red toga in the breakers —
in the affected company of fat-arsed senators
he could be blessed wading the volumes of his white body
through the still fresh waters of his marble swimming bath

The sighing

travelling through a heedless landscape dark with snow
enclosed by grey's weight
all day long monks trekking past
on mulishlean mules
converted crows across the stripped blue earth
on the road to Italy and culture
              and the Pope's ring
all great spirits travel South
to bring back yearnings

but we in our snorting car
search for battlefields and places of death
and the sweet oblivion of snow

if I never again walk
in the whispering whistling shade of the Stambos[4] oaks
never again hear the toads
cracking their necknuts
I don't mind

want so is die lewe
that's life
c'est la vie

where does it lead, this maze of roads?
the snow remains deaf as a post

(7th April 1967 — Verdun)

Morning song

(for Uys Krige and Paul van Ostayen)

Good morning crack of day and darkness, foetus of light
your little hands and hair licked smooth
your silver heart reverberating!
        'morning sight

'Morning mighty rugged land
wearing tree and animal on your sleeve
granting the sky a place to stand!
        'morning form

'Morning kafferpruim tree[5] giving your heart's blood
to breadrolls, bougainvillea o don't mourn,
thorn tree lick your ribs clean!
        'morning colour

'Morning blue crane forever clearing your throat,
honey-bill go'way bird, rock-pigeon tree-shade,
swallow and hotnotsgod[6], muscovy duck cackling away!
        'morning imagery

'Morning ant you itching birthmark of the night,
'morning dam full of fish, 'morning goat, say good-morning ox,
'morning palm tree, green bones in the sky!
        'morning discovery

'Morning sun and clouds far behind nerves
behind visions of silver blood —
how's it going at the other end of the world?
        pithache, you up already?

Good morning, you who scoop out everything fresh when you see
and experience in colour, take long strides across the solid earth
to fly up with a clatter of bones
            : and topple shattered as this knowledge launches from
                                                you.

                                        (Ezulwini)

29

The hand full of feathers[7]

ma
    I've been thinking
if I ever come home
it will be without warning towards daybreak
with years of hoarded treasure
on the backs of iron cows

there's still a blueness on the world
sht — softly I open the back-yard gate
old Wagter growls
but then his tail stirs with memory
Fritz Kreisler plays something sweet on his violin
ma knows
a few Viennese waltzes of course
and amazed the windows start listening
people whom I don't know at all
lean out in nightrobes full of smiles and elbows
people whose laps I peed on when I was small
inside ma's heart comes to a standstill
(and where are the glasses?)
pa wakes up with a start, stupefied
but ma is already outside
in red cheeks and a dressing gown

And I'm standing there large as life
on the lawn next to the small cement pond
where the new outhouses have been added on
           somewhat worn by the long journey
wearing a top hat
a smart suit
carnation in the jacket
new Italian shoes for the occasion
my hands full of presents
a song for my ma a bit of pride for my own pa

but ma knows it's me all the same
and behind me my caravan
as befits an overseas traveller
my wife and children dressed up in bow-ties
each with three Boland[8] words in the mouth
my musicians
the rifle bearers
friends comrades
political advisors
and road-managers
a debtor or two

just this side of the vineyard there grows a tame rose
goodness but the air is crisp
there comes pa too what's up
just like that on an empty stomach
the mountains have turned grey
the oaktrees have thickened
but never mind

                    ma
I've been thinking I'll be there anyway
like a Coloured choir on Christmas morning
ma
I've been thinking how we'll cry then
and drink tea

It seems blind Wagter couldn't wait
he's dead, apparently. . .
perhaps Fritz Kreisler won't take to such a long trip. . .
but if he can't come
I'll hire Paganini. . .
sleep soundly, one ear cocked:
unlike old Thinksomuch[9]
wherever I plant a little feather
a squawking chicken will spring up!

The blood on the doorposts

old poet
come
break the unleavened bread
take the water
this meal will bring you enlightenment

you ask
look-out on the walls of the city
judge of the unnumbered hours
when the day will again fall open?

know then
that somewhere else it is always day
only you are blind
and the shadows obstructing our world
are hills
are birds

the crab bursts from its carapace
let your cancer rise out of you, blossoming
throw up your soul
take your own death
because your blood will wash you
whiter than snow whiter
than the first daybreak

come
be the pass-over lamb
give me your stunted hand
bend down
recognize the final black rose
and say
to hell with the whole damned lot
and then die leaving your fears behind
let go

because poet across your lunar bed I will pack stones
white as poems
whiter than the beacons of your journey
to keep the poisonous rains of dusk
from discolouring your bones
and the birds of the hills
from chocking on your worms

old poet
come
smear blood on the doorposts
your deliverance is at hand
be glad

Populous death_

(for Jheronimus van Aken) [10]

and then naively the groping hand flowers
its tongue, its stick full of little hairs:
to evoke a creation —
the lacquered world and filleted flesh
the pure excretion of skinned fears
the counting and recounting of hell's delights

how they grimace and spill
about the human spoke:
man —
for all things spring forth from the manmade
small people naked as eggs
swollen up like mirrors
singled out to rot —
the illusion that is life
belches forth as caesar christ sot

hardened under paint's thin hide
there now lies the heart of a painting:
this selfsame gestate death —
tracks and trails from the bloodripe brush
to the boil of the mouth's clapper sealed
in a single rearing
rictus of violence

come
green Jerome:
give me —
a wormy kiss

from

Lotus [1]

1970

Ek is bevrees ek verlang aldag meer na 'n 'eéwording

Ek is bevrees ek verlang aldag meer na 'n éénwording,
'n integrasie-deur-die-liefde, met 'n god. Ek sê
,bevrees' omdat ek 'n agnostikus is, nooit kan glo
in die bestaan van gode nie, aangewys is daarop om
god-in-mens te soek en te soek. Is dit waarom ek
smag na daardie mistieke huwelik?
Ek is bevrees ek verlang al hoe meer na 'n éénwording,
'n desintegrasie-deur-die-liefde, met 'n god. A-haa,
maar nie enige hierjy god nie! Ek
wil 'n god hê wat na semen en knoffel ruik, wat deur
berge en waters breek, wat feilbaar en wreed en
menslik en afskuwelik is, lieflik soos 'n granaatbos
in die silwer naag, vet en met die kop van 'n olifant,
'n krygsman, 'n minnares, 'n hermafrodiet, 'n god met
'n skaduwee en dou op haar skouers wat dae lank hoog
in die populierboom die flaminke in hul vlug sit en tel
en die grassade laat ritsel waar sy loop

,,Laat jou skerp borsies mý bors deurboor
En met jou onpeilbare seks, verslind myne!"

Want Sjiwa is my soort van god. En ek is bevrees ek
sal aanhou loop langs stowwerige paaie of deur
modder in die winter, al langs die pelgrimroetes,
selfs daar waar die Ganges haar gang gaan totdat
ek daardie god trillend in my voel, totdat ek op
my knieë daardie goddelike orgasme ontkéten voél
en nie meer een is nie, en ook nie twee nie.
Want die aanbidder en die god is een en as jy die
god ken bekén jy jou self. Jy moet jouself liefhê
soos jou naaste.

,,Hy lei my van die irreële na die reële
Van die duisternis na die lig . . .
Sjiwa! Sjiwa!"

,,Kom na my toe. En nou gaan ek Jou die Groot Waarheid
vertel. Jy gaan Jou in my verlief, Jy gaan na my
honger en dors, sonder my gaan Jy onrustig wees.
Dan gaan Jy my soek en Jy gaan na my toe kom. En
dan eers gaan Jy vry wees, vry! Vry soos 'n god!"

I am afraid and each day yearn more fervently . . .

I am afraid and each day yearn more fervently for union,
an integration-through-love, with a god. I say
'afraid' because I am agnostic, could never believe
in the existence of gods, and am set on seeking
and seeking god-within-man. Is this why I
pine for that mystical marriage?
I am afraid and yearn even more fervently for union,
a disintegration-through-love, with a god. A-haa,
but not any old god! Not one of those
pale Creators or Immaculate Conceptions! I
want to have a god who reeks of sperm and garlic, who
crashes through mountains and waters, fallible and cruel and
human and hideous, exquisite as a pomegranate tree
in the silver night, fat and elephant-headed,
a warrior, a mistress, a hermaphrodite, a god with
a shadow and dew on her shoulders who sits for days on end
high in the poplar tree counting the flamingoes in their flight
causing the grass blades to rustle where she walks

'Let your sharp breasts pierce my breast
And with your unfathomable sex, engulf mind!'

Because Shiva is my kind of god. And I am afraid I will
keep on walking along dusty paths or through
mud in the winter, following the pilgrim routes,
even down where the Ganges goes her way until
I feel that god thrilling within me, until on
my knees I feel that godlike orgasm unshackle
and am no longer one, nor am I two.
For the worshipper and the god are one and if you
know the god then you acknowledge your self. You must love
        yourself
as you do your neighbour.

'He leads me from the unreal to the real,
From darkness to the light. . .
Shiva! Shiva!'

'Come to me. Now I will tell You the Great Truth.
Within me You will fall in love with Yourself, You will
hunger and thirst for me, without me You will be restless.
Then You will seek me and You will come to me. And
only then will You be free, free! Free as a god!

Have you ever seen how the cross spins . . .

have you ever seen how the cross spins
and the lips grin on the sky?

behind the mountains there harbours an eye
whitestar above makes a wide-open house

reality was just a boundary a rumour

(the essence of death is jealousy)

I will practice well what I learnt in the east so as to reach you more swiftly. What did I learn in the east? Shut up for three years in a room without light I learnt to walk like the wind. My eyes are walking-sticks feeling for stars, because stars are only stones. I will rise up in rebellion and go home. You will see me when I am still a great way off and water will stream across your cheeks so that I can wash the dust from my body. And when we have eaten the fatted calf you will come and lie on my breast and ask what did you bring with? Death I'll say. You walked a long way to find death? Yes but now I know it's mine. But when you left death stayed behind; now that you are back it is here again, I feel him restful in my body like a shadow in the night. Then I will jump up and smash all the plates and chuck out the wine and scream: Death! you renounced me!

Death! you slut!

Deadstill you stand in the night . . .

Deadstill you stand in the night and your ears sort out
the sounds — like a dog snuffling under a crust of flies
until he reaches the scrap of meat; then you hear
the anxious rhythms of love. First from the
flat just above your head, then from next door, from down
below, and so on — variations on the same clopping,
the same pacing up and down of the animal
in the cage in all the similar flats, along all the
corridors behind every wall, in the dark cavities
of each of these identical blocks of flats. People
are making love. Knead and gnaw and heave. Like a
submarine crew trapped at the bottom of the sea
hammering against the broadsides trying to make contact
with *anything* in the lifeless chaos surrounding them. The
whistling sounds of feather mattresses[11], bedposts
fretting against the walls, the uncertainty, the
urgency, the hesitation as positions are changed,
the stamina — keep up, perhaps I'll even reach
orgasm. And with your ears you see the sweat,
the balled fists and eyes staring wide or latched
fast, with your ears you see the rancid taste in the
mouth and the last exists, the lucid hot
landscapes in your head where you try to be present
without your body — because your body is elsewhere, strung
rhythmically onto the fine wire of darkness and wait and
pray that that wire might snap and the body
hurtle broken into the gulley of light.
Then again when you lie deadstill in the ground, lie
chewing on your tongue where it's shadow, and listen to the
rhythm which is life up above: wind, trees, day-and-night
— the piping sounds of love and love-making.
Because now you yourself are seed.

That's the answer . . .

That's the answer: to be an old man, a naked
treedweller, too old to climb down to the ground, too deaf
to hear how the birds scoff and cackle — a greybeard
who plasters his shoulderblades with leaves and believes these
to be feathers — and to live in such a way that you can have
intercourse with the darkness and the leaves turn yellow in
the autumn.

(when the house flaps like this)

flowers will not bloom again this season
the sky has puffed up stiff and blue
as a bruised cheek the hollow buildings
shimmer and smell wet we look
through the window at the brooms of rain
autumn autumn is in the house white with our breath

watermelons and plums and sun and radishes
are now subjects we discuss between frozen sheets
we drag our attention back to the hills
hips of women a fear
an oppression come over the ridges the rosy trees o
autumn autumn is in the flag black with our breath

(womanway)

I translate, and adapt:
from the elemental Sahara:

I walked with the pilgrims,
wandering between holy shrines —
but nothing is more holy than your body —
here are the sanctified Januna and mother Ganges,
here Prayaga and Benares, here are Sun and Moon

I dreamed together with exiles
wandering between shadows of memories
but nothing offers more safety than your body —
here are the desecrated Cape and Mountains of Tears,
here are Langa and Nyanga[12], histories change to truth

translate me o and adapt me
to the elemental Sahara

(the feast of falling apart)

stripped naked before the court of angels
hand cupped in front of the commas of the flesh
— those which at a touch want to be exclamation marks —
when we sink, chastising ourselves with ecstasy and fear

(the honour of thieves)

the nights are not ours
and already the days are stripped grey —
nonetheless we must be good to each other,
mutilated, fused with cold in the dark
gulfs between sheets

I also want to be doused like you. . .

I also want to be doused like you
the cat
lies asleep on its ribcase and the night
surrounds the lamp-poles, fire blows

in the corpses of my words my hands
dip into the water that they may recover
and grow
my wife
you are lying asleep on

your ribcase it's five minutes to three, I also want
to hear my friends walking through the silkthistles
their soft laughter whirring up into the trees

like starlings
a jewish wedding under the fig trees
and there's no more beer in the fridge
HAA the silence o o o o o o

from

Oorblyfsels

(Remnants)

1970

Please don't feed the animals

ek is Germaans
ek is wreed
ek is blank
ek sluip uit die oerbos van mites
en sagas
en staan geroepe en vasberade
en voorbestem
op die vlaktes
van hierdie chaotiese kontinent
regop
luister
ek is Germaans
ek is wreed
regverdigheid is nooit maklik
verdelg alle afwyking
ek grawe die oog uit die nag
die skande van nonwhite inheemsheid
tas my nooit aan
son en liefde word geweer
deur my skaamtevliese
die skild van my huid
my white badge of courage
luister
ek weet
ek is
ek is Germaans
ek is wreed
ek ken my Saterdag en my Sondag
ek weet hoe dit moet
en wanneer
my saad is bleek
ek is die oog in die nag
ek kom met my Saracens vol beskawing
met my stralers vol vooruitgang
ek irrigeer die woestyn
en tem die natural resources
ek suig die olie uit die aarde
en bou latrines op die maan
luister
en beef
ek is Germaans

lease don't feed the animals

am Germanic
am cruel
am white
steal from the primordial forest of myths
nd sagas
nd stand called upon and resolute
nd predestined
pright
n the plains
f this chaotic continent
sten
am Germanic
am cruel
ghteousness is never easy
estroy all deviants
dig out the night's eye
he disgrace of being born non-white
ever moves me
un and love don't rifle
y membrane of shame
he shield of my hide
y white badge of courage
sten
know
am
am Germanic
am cruel
know my Saturday and my Sunday
know how it should be
nd when
y seed is pale
am the eye in the night
come with my Saracens full of culture
y jets full of progress
irrigate the desert
nd tame the natural resources
suck the oil from the earth
nd construct latrines on the moon
sten
nd tremble
am Germanic

49

ek is wreed
ek het afkoms
ek stam
ek is suiwer ek is eng
so soos blank
ek sien
ek oordeel
ek skep
ek lei my blinde Teutoniese God
soos 'n wit olifant
aan die wit slurp
deur die wit en heidense duisternis
ek is Afrikaans
ek breek
oop
pasop!
olifante onthou . . .

wees bly aan my voetbank

laat dit jol

I am cruel
I have parentage
I am part of the tree
I am pure I am strait
much like whiteness
I see
I judge
I create
I lead my blind Teutonic God
like a white elephant
by its white trunk
through the white and pagan darkness
I am Afrikaans
I break
open
watch out!
elephants remember . . .

be content at my foot-rest

have a ball

from

Skryt

(Write/Cry)

1972

Bagamayo

as jy die sand van 'n vreemde land lek
wanneer jy daar op besoek aankom
dan verwerp jy sy bose geeste en kwale

my kokosneut, die son, onthaal die ganse uitspansel,
my vader het twee messe aan my oorhandig: ek gebruik een
maar die ander glip uit my vuis: dis die aarde en die hemel

toe die maan daar bo 'n melkkoei tussen die kalwers was
het ek jou uit die binneland probeer bereik
net soos eertydse karavane: die kamele met hul rûe so vol pyn

langs die paaie uit die hart lê baie skedels,
dis die bakens van die reis,
al die paaie uit die duister skitter deur die lyf

die swart slawe hang in die boom: so is die eiervrug,
'n wit Arabier staan een-been gestoel: die sampioen bid,
onderweg het ek'n ketting sien lê maar wie tel die wit miere op?

waar sal Bagamayo aan die lippe raak? oor die see
sleep die een dooie siel die ander: 'n dhow en haar seil
sing soos 'n baie ou Swahili-lied:

> wees bly, my siel, laat alle sorge gaan
> binnekort bereik ons die plaas van jou verlangens
> die stad van palmbome, Bagamayo.
> toe ek ver was, hoe seer was my hart
> by die gedagte aan jou, my pêrel
> my oord van geluk, Bagamayo.
>
> daar kam die vroue hulle hare
> jy kan die hele jaar palmwyn drink
> in die tuin van liefde, Bagamayo.
> die dhows kom aan met vloeiende seile
> om die weelde van Uleias in te skeep
> in die hawe van Bagamayo.

Bagamayo

if you lick the sand
when you come on a visit to a strange land
then you ward off its fevers and evil spirits

my coconut, the sun, entertain the entire firmament,
my father handed me two knives: I use one
but the other slips from my fist: heaven and earth

when the moon up above was a cow between calves
I tried to reach you from the interior
like the old-time caravans: the camels with their backs so full of
pain

many skulls line the paths from the heart,
marking out the voyage
all paths from the gloom glitter through the body

the black slaves hang in the tree: such is the eggfruit
a white Arab perches on one leg: the mushroom prays,
I saw a chain lying along the way but who picks up the white ants?

where will Bagamayo touch the lips? across the sea
one dead soul drags the other: a dhow and her sail
sing like a very old Swahili song:

> be glad, my soul, forget all cares
> we will soon reach the place that you have yearned for
> the city of palm trees, Bagamayo
> when I was far off, how my heart ached
> with thoughts of you, my pearl
> my region of joy, Bagamayo.
>
> there the women comb out their hair
> you can drink palm wine the whole year round
> in the garden of love, Bagamayo
> the dhows approach with flowing sails
> to load up with the wealth of Uleias
> in the harbour of Bagamayo

55

o, wat 'n genot is dit om die ngomas te sien
waar die fraaiste meisies swaaiend dans
as dit aand is in Bagamayo.
wees stil my hart, alle sorge is vergeet.
die dromme bons van vreugde
ons kom aan in Bagamayo.

o, my hart, waar is jou tong? want hier lê die Bagamayo
van geslagte slawe in kettings uit Afrika gesleep
om van die hand gesit te word in die mensemark van Zanzibar

hier groei 'n klip en daar groei 'n klip: die grafte
en die koei in die hemel se uier is vol spykers
en met my mes kan ek die kokosson nooit breek

die oseean spoel soos bloed teen hierdie land,
ek staan op my knieë waar die harte neergelê is
met die sand soos onverteerbare klagtes in die keel

nou weet ek waarom die miere aan die aarde kleef

o, what a joy to see the ngomas
where the most graceful girls sway in dance
when evening falls in Bagamayo
be still my heart, all cares are forgotten:
the drums throb with delight
we are drawing closer to Bagamayo

O, my heart, where is your tongue? for here lies the Bagamayo
of generations of slaves dragged from Africa in chains
disposed of in Zanzibar's human bazaar

a stone grows here, a stone grows there: the graves
and in heaven the cows udder is full of nails
and with my knife I could never split the coconutsun

the ocean washes like blood against this land,
I stand on my knees where the hearts are laid down
sand in my throat like grievances that cannot be stomached

now I know why the ants cleave to the earth

Hoe vaak was ons hier tussen koeltes op die vloer. . .

hoe vaak was ons hier tussen koeltes op die vloer
die reuk van terpentyn en van vuur
die doeke is wit want die oë is leeg
die afsydigheid van die nag
en die maan 'n glimlag buite jewers
buite sig
die dae vergaan soos seisoene by die ruite
'n wolk, 'n gesig, reënblare, dié gedig,
ek wou my afdruk op jou laat
ek wou jou brandmerk met die vuur
van alleen wees
geen vuur sing so mooi
soos die silwer as van jou bewegings nie
en jou treurige liggaam
ek wou daardie treurigheid uit jou haal
sodat jou liggaam oop mag breek
soos 'n stad oopgaan
op'n helder landskap
vol duiwe en die vuur van bome
en waar silwer kraaie ook onsigbaar is in die nag
en die maan 'n mond wat mens aan die brand kan steek
en dan wou ek hê dat jy kon lag
en jou bitter lyf
my hande van porselein op jou heupe
jou asem so 'n donker pyn
'n swaard is aan my oor
hoe dikwels was ons hier
waar net silwer skaduwees nog roer
alleen deur jou moet ek myself verwerp
deur jou alleen het ek besef hoe haweloos ek is
in 'n brandende see

How drowsy we were here wrapped in coolness . . .

how drowsy we were here wrapped in coolness on the floor
the smell of turpentine and fire
the fabrics white to our empty eyes
the indifference of the night
and the moon a smile somewhere outside
out of sight
days fall apart like seasons at the panes
a cloud, a face, leaves of rain, this poem,
I want to leave my print on you
I want to brand you with the fire
of solitude
no fire sings clear
as the silver ash of your movements
and your sad body
I wished to draw that sadness from you
that your body might break open
like a city opening
onto a bright landscape
filled with pigeons and the fire of trees
where silver crows are also out of sight in the night
and the moon a mouth that one can ignite
and then I wished that you could have laughed
and your bitter body
my hands of porcelain on your hips
your breath such a dark ache
a sword at my ear
how often were we here
where only silver shadows are left stirring
alone through you I must refuse myself
through you alone I realize I have no harbour
in a burning sea

Dar es-Salaam : harbour of peace

Dar es-Salaam: it's when night is darkest,
just before morning, that the muezzin calls the faithful
because they are all asleep
and his sad complaint flies over minaret forefingers,
        rooftops and lovers and flowers and docks
and his sad complaint dawns over the city

one proverb goes: 'the cock that crows at night
                        without waiting for daybreak
brings misfortune, slaughter it immediately'; but according to a
                                            second:
'it is unwise to react when you are called
only once in the heart of the night'

you can let that bird loose as often as the sun:
but it always returns
— I think of you, brothers in exile, with only bitterness
                                        for earth

the day comes to dig a sweet earth: a sea full of ships and shells and
                                            coral,
the shells so young they're white — beaches,
and coconut palms very proud and slender with small firm breasts,
banana plantations, mangoes and paw-paws;
the city has sparkling clouds and crows weep in the wind,
'caw! caw!' prophecy the windpolished whitebreasts,
the other birds whistle through their wings: to whistle, so the
                                        saying goes,
is to call on the devil:
under fans in offices sit bureaucrats
with boils on their lips and flies on their hands:
'wash clothes without water and you invite poverty'

I think of you, freedom-fighters, with the thin vomit
                of a present that cannot be stomached
with weapons and fear somewhere far out on the foggy borders —
'if a man bites you rub chickenshit into the wound
and his teeth will rot'

with low tide and dusk the Indians come down to the sea
the moon a pale conch glistening in the creases of the void
where stars also swim —
to chat, savour the low tide and the twilight
and grow quieter, sitting cross-legged
and when it's dark enough
seek out an India far across the waters

I think of you, exiled brothers struggling with us for freedom,
I think of you who try to follow the sun:
if you point at the new moon with your finger
then your finger will be cut, but the finger
that picks out the moon is no moon
and if you blow over the pustules on your hands
then it is the moon which becomes a wart

I have heard: 'he who eats chicken's feet will become a wanderer';
'if you walk bare-headed under the moon your brain will dry up
and one day you will go crazy';
'a lunatic who always enjoys his meals
will never regain understanding'

Ukichomeka kisu ndani ya ala anaposema mwenye
kigugumizi basi hataweza kuendelea na kusema tena:[13]
'stick a knife in it's sheath while the stutterer talks
and you deprive him of all speech' —
here in Dar es-Salaam night has already fallen

Flame

the fly cannot alight on the lion's blood:
the fire;
    the lady's veil rustles and pines:
a flame;
laid by fire behind and around the lips of the universe,
blinding and terrible
breaks through the brushwood
splitting each tree into tree and shadow
scorching the white worms in the eyes:
sunrise over Africa

I see
not visions but revelations and recognitions,
I seek this place;   our silver jet balances over its shadow
like a watch-hand crossing uncoded cyphers of time,
our aircraft passes dwellings and the Nile is the sand-snake
and the fire captures the sky

in Khartoum the wind is the desert's bloody breath:
'Above, through a sky terrible in its stainless beauty',
(flames allow no blemish) 'and the splendours
of a pitiless blinding glare', (the eyes' gaze leaves no imprint)
'the simoon caresses you like a lion
with a flaming breath. . .
the very skeletons of mountains. . .' etc.:   *Sir Richard Burton*

General Gordon Pasha's consumed head fruits on a spear:
teeth grinning white clenched against the light
teeth black with the fire's countenance and the tongue is ash —
that vengeance burns clean —
while the Mahdi's men
with flickering turbans
            diminish like corpses across the flats

south of here the Kabaka's wives sit
in their huts and belch, fat with beestings
further south the graceful galloping of giraffe:
bundles of kindling are hoisted,
and high against slopes of the mountain of fire
where the hoar snow begins
lies the coalblack body of the leopard

Africa, so often pillaged, purified, burnt!
Africa stands in the sign of fire and flame. . .

Exile, representative

for F.M. and M.K.

you grow less agile, more compliant
fat comes heaping onto your body
like ants deep inside a dead animal
one day you are finished off
your eyes burn all the more desolate

you live as if you'd never die
because this is not where you lead your life
yet death walks in your body
death comes down the trails of your guts
death is knotted into your wings

and holes form in the earth behind your eyes
the hills grow silent, their greenness fades
hands and smiles cave in
photographs and pamphlets are pasted
over memories: *experience is a dream*

you learn to beg
and feed the raw contrition of your people
to the insatiable bureaucrats
and all Officials of the World's Conscience
you look into the gaps of their hearts: deep into the mirror

so that in the morning you are still awake
with a grey mutter in your mouth
words swarming
like parasites around your tongue
and in your throat your words make nests

you're a full-time fugitive in the crowd
you don't smoke you don't drink
because your life is a weapon
you die miserably poisoned by despair
shot down like a dog in a dead-end street

and by the time you want to smash the day with your fist
and say: look my people are rising up!
here it comes, blinding! *Maatla!*[14]
you've forgotten the silences of the language
ants creep from the cry
from belching entrails come blind freedom fighters

from

Met Ander Woorde

(In other Words)

1973

Om jou aan jouself te wend...

om jou aan jouself te wend
is moeilik

nou die dood
na mens se oë begin soek

is daar alleen een gretige voorneme
om sterker te word einde toe

jy voel jy sluit jou aan
by 'n ondergrondse beweging

To harness yourself. . .

to harness yourself
is hazardous

now that death
begins to seek out the eyes

a single burning purpose remains
to grow stronger towards the end

you feel you are bound to yourself
by an underground movement

The taste of void. . .

the taste of the void

the world is a bizarre place:

hardly on your feet and evening falls

When the canopy of sky tears. . .

when the canopy of sky tears
then all the stars fall out:
'you know you can't let a drunk man
                            work on the roof!'

And when you're old and rigid. . .

and when you're old and rigid
as a cleft stick —
below ground the water waits
like a mirror

When I die. . .

when I die
place a locust of jade
between my lips, another in my mouth

that's the word
a voracious pest
which gnawed sense down to stubble

such is the horse-fly
in a high wooden tower
such is the iceberg teeming with ants

from

'n Seisoen in die Paradys

(A Season in Paradise)

1976

Ek sal sterf en na my vader gaan. . .

ek sal sterf en na my vader gaan
Wellington toe met lang bene
blink in die lig
waar die kamers swaar en donker is
waar sterre soos seemeeue sit op die nok
en engele vir wurms spit in die tuin,
ek sal sterf en met min bagasie in die pad val
die Wellingtonse berge oor
tussen die bome en die skemer deur
en na my vader gaan;

die son sal in die aarde klop
die wind se branders laat die voeë kraak
ons hoor die huurders
skuurloop bo ons kop,
ons sal dambord speel op die agterstoep
— ouvader kul —
en oor die radio
luister na die nag se nuus

vriende, medesterwendes,
moenie huiwer nie; nou hang die lewe
nog soos vlees om ons lywe
maar die dood beskaam nie;
ons kom en ons gaan
is soos water uit die kraan so
soos klanke uit die mond
soos ons kom en ons gaan;
ons béne sal die vryheid kén —
kom saam
            in my sterf in in my na my vader gaan
Wellington toe waar die engele
met wurms vet sterre uit die hemel hengel;
laat ons sterf en vergaan en vrolik wees:
mý vader het 'n groot bôrdienghuis

I will die and go to my father

I will die and go to my father
in Wellington[15] on long legs
dazzling in the light
where the rooms are heavy and dark
where stars sit like seagulls on the rooftop
and angels dig for worms in the garden
I will die, pack up a few things
                              take the road
across the Wellington mountains
through the trees and the twilight
and go to my father;

the sun will pound in the earth
the joints will creak with waves of wind
we'll hear the lodgers
scraping around overhead
and play draughts on the back porch
— what a cheat, old father —
and listen to the night's news
on the radio

friends, fellow mortals,
don't tremble; life still hangs
like flesh from our bodies
but death has no shame —
we come and we go
like water from a tap
like sounds from the mouth
like our comings and goings:
it's our bones which will know freedom
come with me
                    bound in my death, to my father
in Wellington where the angels
use worms to fish fat stars from heaven;
let us die and decompose and be merry:
my father has a large boarding-house

Journey
(: I have died a little)

1.

ringing out from our blue heavens[16]
but our heavens are charged with leaping fires
in the trees that slant up against the mountain
a silver light and other things which blind the eyes
a sudden taste like the electric shock of what has
no beginning and no end
: I have died a little

from our deep seas breaking round[17]
the sea no longer has sympathy for the white man
the scum spreads from Europe
oil tankers in their thousands like festering whales
the milkwood stands utterly twisted with fear
nothing rinses the rot out any longer
: I have died a little

valleys and plains and then only flies
and then the desert
in the desert you have no need for a name
you are your own name
you are the nameless one
God, engulf us!
: I have died a little

when the fire burns out the hills are scorched black
to the edge of the night
go lead your eyes between the stars
like water between trees spitting blossoms
and the wind shakes loose concealing nothing
the wind empty houses
: I have died a little

game-reserves for the animals of the land
homelands for tame people
we saw a man in rags following the trail
without descent or refuge spools of flesh on a skeleton
a native an inland exile endlessly moving
deeper inward there was room enough in his eyes
: I have died a little

come all you gods like squawking chickens
unity is strength
farms townships towns suburbs
cities where music gets a grip
and dogs which know nothing but Afrikaans
born and bred to claw people open
: I have died a little

my land my land o anus full of blood
and love like a stiff body within the body. . .
that day we rode out like the blind
crossing the land again and again
the flames of the sky licking through the panes
we are blue and dying and life lies outside
    I have died a little

2.

the day rises in the east
from behind the blue mould of white breakers
from the soft sugar-cane plantations
the day is light

all things which inhabit the skies
and are born out of light
below on earth
belong to people

in the mountains there are no longer gods
at night the moon is an empty house
the gods have always been human
our love is a kingdom of the gods

the day raises all the mountains
and goes like fire through the desert
our people stagger drunk with light
each one taking shelter in his own shadow

across the rank towers of the city
across the white trees of the farms
one human being screams out *oo-aa*
and another replies

across climates and seasons
across sorrows and harvests
across flat lands and slopes
and hunter and grass

the day blows
until evening falls
until the cold sea
and the coast of the dead are reached

the night rises high in the east
like breakers rolling towards the land
engulfing vineyards and orchards
the day that butterfly unable to swim

oo-aa one human being screams outside
and another human being replies
grace grace grace revealed in this place
death is the blood in our veins

3.

such is man
such is his striving to be human
pressing for love
and acceptance by his fellows
you call and hear no echo

there will be a massacre
blood from the gardens and streets
firebrands freedom flags,

vultures across the bright floors
in the air-conditioned hotel lounges
smiles split eyes threaded onto a silver needle
there are beetles in the soup

soldiers by the lorry-load children on the roof-tops
a white god floating white in the bunker up above
cries shots the screech of teeth

e great pink animals stockinged up to the knees
e cows chew on carcasses houses burst into dust
ens moan,

d the mine-shafts are taken over by ants
the factories the orange-trees turn grey
u call and do not hear
ch is man, o my love,
u call and do not hear
ch is death this blood in our veins:
edom or death,

from the Cape to Rio[18]

a great and bitter and dry land. . .
a land where the earth shudders and jolts
and volcanic mountains have just grown cold. . .

Table Mountain the prow against which the oceans foam
above the crest the white sails blow

because the wind rises
the rigging sings with wind
and like butterflies from an Eastern verse —
but the breakers here are so much higher,
the desert and the wilderness much closer
to the body
there is little refinement
no kings grieving over empires
the only cosmetic the white blind
                    of death —
and yet, like butterflies from a light poem
the yachts shoot out, seeking pleasure beyond the Bay:
the *Old Glory, Jacaranda, Concorde,*
Albatros, Rangoon Lady, Westwind
Outburst, Impala, Buccaneer, Zwerver,
L'Orgueil, Golden City, Silver Streak
and *Dabulamanzi* — 'he-who-cleaves-the-water'

boats and wings and flags sails birds
                    to Rio

past Robben Island[19]

where prisoners can no doubt hear the sails
flap against the sun
where eyes probe so often and so far
into the sun
that like water they can follow
the dots of freedom to the horizon
where they dream that someone anyone
will drain off the water
so that the people can pass dry-shod over False Bay
to the great and promised land
where they dream of the voyage
from Robben Island to the Cape. . .

brownburnt youngsters set the sails
and turn over the breakers
                    there is a pulse and tremor
like the rhythms of a poem
            skirting Robben Island and past, and past
flash *Old Glory, Jacaranda, Concorde*. . .

ashpale old men bend down
            count and arrange the grains of salt:

Sometime last night, I'm not sure how late . . .

sometime last night, I'm not sure how late,
half-way between Satur and Sunday,
the sea parted before me,
a word changes to thought,
our sea, my sea, sea, a blue
pitching raucous sea
white with excitement —
the breakers glass locomotives
filled with water
smashing themselves mindlessly
to smithereens on the beach;

I am a god and the sun never sinks
the sea never sinks
sometimes it darkens just along the edge,
from a far off yesterday I sent for my friends
to share this transfiguration with me —
Daan, John, Ampie, Faan:
'to come and squat here in the sand —
will will not hear
the aeroplane wait
above the roar of the sea's rejoicing'

— and perhaps it was already too late

Stranger. . .

Stranger,
        when you pause here for a heart-beat
with a cold eye
on a whispering wind-cleansed morning/when the trees shake
and the sun a blue bird falls through the sky —
then listen intently:

I myself had no voice
I was merely a vocal-chord old as breath
borrowed from the people tightly fastened to a heart
brilliant and pivotal as the grave,
and what I had to say was simply to give
to that which caused me to resonate

listen well
with your ear to the ground
the rebellion steps up
to make the world round/listen
that's the sun singing in every corn-ear
praising peasant and labourer,
listen well to the way the wind quivers —
the earth stinks of righteousness

listen well
and then go your own way:
no one can suppress death
and it's in you that something of us lives on

(Onrus)[20]

deadsure I believe in a hereafter:
I will die and attired in my paradise robes
        I will come down here
to have a holiday
        here
where the sun lies like a carpet
over everything
    so I can follow this road
to the place where the milkwood
and the rooikrans[21] grow
        against the vibrant sky
the mountain there against the sea rising up
behind the lane

I will live with the cats in the coppice
and walk through the walls
through time which now and then jells into substance
until it flows on and rots into life
and when you come here to take a rest
I will sit goggling[22]
in your company
and go looking for biscuits in the cake-tin at night
(don't blame the mouse)

and I won't bother you
but you will know that I am here
                because
by day I will make the sea green and blue
and by night I will light up the stars
with my eyes

First prayer for the hottentotsgod [23]

they say, little beast, little creator, the elders say
that the fields of stars, the earth-dwellers and all things
that turn and rise up and sigh and crumble
were brought forth by you, that you planted an ostrich-feather
in the darkness and behold!   the moon!
o most ancient one,
                    you who fired by love
consume your lover, what led you to forsake
the children of those — the human stuff —
remember?   summoned by you
from the mud?
there are fires in the sky, mother, and the moon
cold as a shoe, and a black cry like smoke
mixed with dust — for your black people, people maker, work
like the dust of knives in the earth that the money
might pile up elsewhere
for others --
grassyellow lady of prayer,
                              hear our smoke and our dust —
chastise those who debased your people to slavery

87

This thing has the requisite length. . .

this thing has the requisite length
and as for form it looks
(cock-eyed though it may be) as it should

since it lies flat we will not be able
to gauge its thickness;

what strikes the eye in the first place is is —
I mean the fitful pulsing motion
which insists on denying beginning and end

and in this way, spurning references outside itself
proclaims an autonomous — hence enigmatic? — existence

what would be audible if eyes could still hear
are in the second place kindred sounds
because rhythm, or rather, subsidiary parts

which care for each other
are the small signs of organic life

certain elements are perhaps repeated
although this is also to plug the gaps
and so rip the *meaning* from its context

but in this way the illusion
of completion is achieved

e.g. the elevated and previously revealed white self
returns and now leads a fervent existence

so take this thing between thumb and heart
hold it skewed against the flow of light
and then name it, you might as well: a poem

Just as when you're tired . . .

just as when you're tired
and stretch out on your back
under the tall tree
with your weapons in the dust

and see how the evening
draws the birds to the tree
until the branches
swarm with stars

and how the moon yellow
on her back her hair
like rays of light around her
drowns in the night

until blinded by tears
and the morning sun you don't see
how the birds fly up
to devour the corpse

that's how your death stretches out:
waiting within you:
a chiming stillness:
a miracle

Prison poems [24]

1975-77

Taalstryd

'Clean as the conscience of a gun' — Miroslav Holub

Ons is oud.
Ons taal is 'n grys reserwis van meer dan honderd jaar
met die vingers styf om die snellers —
en wie sal soos óns kan sing
wanneer ons nie meer daar is nie?
Soos in ons lewe sal ons die aarde verwerp
en die wonderwerke van die vlees wat groei
soos woorde spoel en klop —
Júlle sal die liggame vir ons gedagtes wees
en lewe om ons sterwe te herdenk
en die wysies uit ons beenfluite te tower . . .

Van die struktuur van ons gewete
en uit die skure van ons liefdadigheid
het ons vir julle swart konstruksies laat bou, bliksems —
skole, klinieke, poskantore, polisiestasies —
en nou waai die pluime swart rook
met die klop en die spoel van 'n hart.

Maar julle het nie mooi verstaan nie.
Die Taal moet julle nog bemeester
Ons sal julle die ABC van vooraf voorsê,
ons sal julle tou-wys-maak
mét die riglyne van ons Christelike Nasionale Opvoeding . . .

Julle sal leer om gehoorsaam te wees,
gehoorsaam en onderdanig.
En julle sal die Taal leer gebruik,
onderdanig sal julle die gebruik
want in óns lê die monde
met die gif in die klop en die spoel van die hart.

Julle is die sout van die aarde —
waarmee sal ons ons sterwe smaak kan gee
as julle nie daar is nie?
Julle sál die aarde bitter en brak en glinsterend maak
van die klank van ons lippe . . .

The struggle for the Taal [25]

'Clean as the conscience of a gun' – Miroslav Holub

We ourselves are aged.
Our language is a grey reservist a hundred years old and more
his fingers stiff around the triggers –
and who will be able to sing as we sang
when we are no longer there?
As we did when alive we will spurn the earth
and the miracles of the flesh which grows
throbbing and flowing like words –
It is you who will serve as bodies for our thoughts
and live to commemorate our death,
you will conjure up tunes from the flutes of our bones. . .

From the structure of our conscience
from the stores of our charity
we had black contraptions built for you, you bastards –
schools, clinics, post-offices, police-stations –
and now the plumes blow black smoke
throbbing and flowing like a heart.

But you have not fully understood.
You have yet to master the Taal.
We will make you say the ABC all over again,
we will teach you the ropes
of Christian National Education . . .

You will learn to be submissive
submissive and humble.
And you will learn to use the Taal,
with humility you will use it
for it is we who possess the mouths
with the poison in the throb and the flow of the heart.

You are the salt of the earth –
with what will we be able to spice our dying
if you are not there?
you will make the earth glint, bitter and brackish
with the sound of our lips. . .

Want ons is Christus se laksmanne.
Ons is op die mure om die lokasies
met die geweer in die een hand
en die masjiengeweer in die ander:
ons, sendelinge van die Beskawing.

Ons bring vir julle die grammatika van geweld
en die sinsbou van verwoesting —
uit die tradisie van ons vuurwapens
sal julle die werkwoorde van vergelding hoor
stotter.

Kyk, ons gee vir julle nuwe monde pasella —
rooi ore om mee te hoor rooi oë om mee te sien al
polsende, rooi monde
om die geheime van ons vrees te mag spuit:
daar waar iedere loodpuntwoord vlieg
sal 'n spraakorgaan oopgebreek word . . .

En julle sal die Taal asseblief leer gebruik,
gehoorsaam sal julle dit gebruik, breek . . .
want ons lê reeds met die doodsroggel
se klop en se spoel
aan die lippe . . .

Óns, ons is oud . . .

For we are Christ's executioners.
We are on the walls around the townships
gun in one hand
machine-gun in the other:
we, the missionaries of Civilization.

We bring you the grammar of violence
and the syntax of destruction —
from the tradition of our firearms
you will hear the verbs of retribution
stuttering.

Look what we're giving you, free and for nothing — new mouths,
red ears with which to hear red eyes with which to see
pulsing, red mouths
so that you can spout the secrets of our fear:
where each lead-nosed word flies
a speech organ will be torn open. . .

And you will please learn to use the Taal,
with humility use it, abuse it . . .
because we are down already, the death-rattle's
throb and flow
on our lips . . .

As for us, we are aged. . .

Vriespunt

Hy staan wydsbeen, die son,
en sy koue druip soos 'n flikkerende keël van ys,
n harige vlam van koue selfs. Dit is 'n sidderende geluid
wat klip geword het. Hy staan wydsbeen met sy rug bak
teen die potblou omsingeling van die hemel en laat die spieël
sien: waarin geen beeld flonker nie
maar slegs 'n blanke konsentrasie.

Teen die badkamer se muur is 'n plaat van staal
met die vloeiende omlynings van bandiete wat moet skeer
maar nooit genoeg duidelikheid kry om keel af te sny nie:
die nekare pols ondergronds. Ek voel die appels van verrotting in my
                    bors
en die treine sluk in my gewrigte.
Nou — ná hoe baie maande van eensame opsluiting?—
Kry ek eersklaps 'n regte spieël in my sel, 'n ware oog
van water; maar onder die bevrore oppervlakte
woon 'n lokvoël: 'n verrimpelde geblekte aap
waarskynlik uit Sjina wat buitensporige gebare bedure
en sy mond plooi in 'n lawwe grimas
wanneer hy my oog vang. Laag op laag, grimas op grynslag
en die grysheid van as. Sy mond is die bloederige donkerheid
van die appel se interieur; om sy oë gerlek is die potblou swamme
'n Ding het in die helderheid kom groei: en ek is nie meer alleen nie
Ek sal my woorde moet tel.

O hoe het dit gebeur? Die winter soos appels
is in die aarde krummelrig en grys. Ook die wind
verfrommel die as, die vodde, koerantwoorde, die kadawers van
                    honde,
patroondoppies, die oop nekare van die strate:
die lyke met derms, vol brommers in die hande gebak.
En bo die grafiek van rook sirkel helikopters met oë van staal.
'n Periskoop hoër uit die blou is die yssplinter.

Freezing point

He stands astride, the sun,
and drips with cold like a flickering ice-cone,
a hairy flame of coldness itself. A trembling sound
turned to stone. He stands astride, his back curved
against the livid surrounding sky and allows the mirror
to see: a place where no image glitters,
nothing but blank concentration.

Against the bathroom wall, a sheet of steel,
holds the flowing outlines of convicts forced to shave
without ever seeing clearly enough to cut their throats:
the jugular has a subterranean pulse. I feel the apples of decay in
           my chest
and in my wrists the jolt of trains.
Now — after how many months of solitary confinement? —
I suddenly get a real mirror in my cell, a true eye
of water; but below the frozen surface
there dwells a stool-pigeon: a wrinkled blanched ape
probably Chinese, making extravagant gestures
and creasing his mouth into an inane grimace
when he catches my eye. Layer on layer, grimace on grin
and the greyness of ash. His mouth has the bloody obscurity
of the apple's interior. Livid fungus is flecked around his eyes.
A thing has come to gorw in the brightness: and I am no longer
    alone.
I will have to count my words.

O how did this happen? The winter like apples
in the earth mouldering and grey. And the wind
crumpling the ash, the rags, the words in the paper, the cadavers of dogs,
bullet-cartridges, the open jugulars of the streets:
the corpses, guts covered with horseflies cupped in the hands.
And above the graphic of smoke circle steel-eyed helicopters.
Rising higher into the blueness the periscope of splintered ice.

Winter 1

It snows thick flakes in my sleep,
and white is the coast and white the sea —
inhospitable, a dismal walk
through the scratchmarks, the crackle and crunch, the slanting
        strokes.

Of grey cement the towns
without inhabitants.
Of grey cement the streets the trees
covered in droplets
like small microphones:
the greyness is picked up and multiplied.

Our neighbours are in the waterpipes' lap and splash
the hairy window panes, eyelashes
over the wet of the iris. Into
the white eye of your reclining body
I will descend.   Your teeth are small snowmen.
I will diminish in the lens.

There are guards with black tongues —
tongues like the festering moon — and silver
machine-guns
in the neck between the torn sea
and the bottomless snow-fields of the interior:
a border-post —

On the hill

From some of the crests rise clumps of trees
— indelible miraculous bloodstains — stuck
to their shifting shadows.
Below the shadows the gravestones, sprouting like bill-boards —
many of his uncles and aunts were planted
in this district, and nothing ever came up.
The epitaphs on each couple's headstone
make a comic dialogue supposedly quoted
from one fictitious bible or another.

The homesteads are always built on the hill-tops;
tilting vines skirt and encircle the slopes,
filling the shy valleys
between the hills. The shadows of small birds
fall layer on layer from the vineleaves.

The heat is suffocating. The two neighbours on the nearby crest —
two brothers with matching pairs of braces — pot
shabby carrier pigeons from their ledge
using automatics fitted with silencers.
Sht! Sht! — and the birds with their sudden red letters
fall like bunches of grapes to the ground,
dripping;   the love-greetings leak out.

On his knees he digs into the grit.
The sweat drips like tears over the bridge of his nose. He uncovers
the remains of a pair of jeans, a checked shirt: these are the clothes
that the writer wore when he wanted to write.
A shadow strokes over his hands and he rapidly
covers the grave: the woman stands astride
balanced against the sun so that he can hear
the small hairy clock stifling the time.

But everywhere under the sand of the hillcrest
are grey relics.
He digs a second hole and discovers a book
with a worn red leather cover
full of ideograms.
Perhaps it was the book of primordial ideas.
(Every hill is a stronghold)

In Rue Monsieur-le-Prince. . .

in Rue Monsieur-le-Prince
coming down the same side
as the Luxembourg gardens, on the left
where the evening sun burns the small twigs
so as to make its nest in the trees
the same side as the Odeon theatre
a honey-comb of freedom
as long ago now as May sixty-eight

in Rue Monsieur-le-Prince
is the restaurant where we will meet
at precisely nine o'clock —
you will recognise me, I'll be wearing a beard once again
even though it may be of cheap silver
and the Algerian boss-cum-cook
with the moustache nesting in his red cheeks
will come and put his arms full of bees around my shoulders
saying
alors, mon frère — ça fait bien longtemps. . .

should we order couscous mouton for two?
I can already taste the small snowyellow grains
and the lump of butter —
and a bottle of pitch dark Sidi Brahim
smacking of the sun and the sea?
and after that what would you say to a thé à la menthe
in the damp scalding glasses decorated with flowers?

hear how the same wind calls
through the ancient Paris streets

'you're the one I love and I'm feeling so good!'

Other poems

ek is geen reisagent

God
ek spreek tot U

bly nou bietjie stil
U met U mond soos 'n bos vol takke en rook
met U tande soos brame
met die vlamme van U tong

stuur nie vir my
ek sal U saak toeterend befoeter
U bevel aanvaarbaar maak
soos 'n gedig

want my bek is te glad
want hulle sal my glo

I'm no travel agent

God
I am appealing to you

calm down a little now
You with Your mouth like a bush full of branches and smoke
with Your teeth like brambles
with the flames of Your tongue

do not send for me
I will foul up Your case with my loud mouth
make Your decree palatable
as a poem

because my tongue is too smooth
because they will believe me

Je s'use

Peace treaty? Truce? The stilling of thought?
The stilling of dream? Dream is the death of the real
Waking is the stilling of dream. To voice awareness
is to abandon (annihilate?) a no man's land. Dream
is no man's land. Peace is no man's land. Life is no
man's land. To dream in anonymity is no man's land. The
anonymous dream. The superfluous trench. Life is the trench
running towards death. Behind the bulwarks of dream. The fortress
of dream. Inviolable in dream. 'Impure! Impure!'
Dream is a white flag and a bell. Surrender: the prize
is no man's land. A no man's land riddled with trenches. Trenches
filled with dreams. Death is man's own land. Island and an-
other man's land. Life and another man's land.

Where I am, my breath is. The awareness cannot
be cloven (But is the spirit a cleft?) You are
a motionless obscure animal which stalks yourself and will
take your own life. When you see yourself all your hairs
stand on end in primordial fear. You have swallowed
the bait of your breath. Trapped in the crotch of the spirit.

Now you know these are only words cowering, sleek and shiny
to meet with approval — yet aggressive, embittered and on
the way to their own destination. The words glance over their
shoulders at you, whether fawning or menacing you
cannot tell. The bandage is twisted from your hands
where the words bulge and flake. Words are of the night.
Words wear dark cloaks as disguise and their fabric
is night. Under cover of night words are
only skeletons; here and there leprous spools of flesh
cleave to the bones, grey in colour and wet as
snot. Words are insects. Words are parasites living
in the wound of experience. Experience does not bleed from
within. Experience is the blood oozing
from the incision; it is not the knife which made the incision.
Words are experience (And language the instrument of sense. . .)
Words butcher sense. Words are the — on sight and an sich —
unwitting and inhuman and unfathomable and abstract
pus of the awareness. A man who speaks is a contaminated
man.

Words are symptoms of disease. A man who lives, communicates.
Therefore life is an infectious and deadly disease. The
man who seeks or initiates communication is lost and
searching for himself. (When you bump into someome like this,
kill him immediately. Because all communica-
tion is contamination). If you discover yourself you are dead.
Nirvana is the exquisite joy of the state of death.

But: the terrible thought concerning death is: that at that
moment you lose death. And if you are dead and realize that
it was not an annihilation, that your consciousness
atomised by every worm and digested molecule penetrates
the world — and at that moment realize that further death
(annihilation) is no longer possible?

If I can only gather myself together again, all the segments
of my body, then I will be able to die. Self-knowledge,
nirvana, that which is dead, is simply the unattainable
fullness-of-being.

You who stole me: give me back! As long as I creep
over the earth, in all directions of the wind, an im-
perialist and an exploiter, that's how long I am doomed to
life, to lack of fulfillment and dissipation and
for just that long the words, those ant-spies which
must seek and drag me back to the anthive of the grave,
will flow from me. My quests are a blind white queen.
My death/my prize is a diaspora of exiles sown
across the world. Death is the homeland of my ancestors.

Physically, therefore, I will not be able to die. My homeland is an
idea. If I can harness myself to a single idea then
I am dead. When I am and know that I am, at one with being, then
I am dead.

The ideal is to be a zombie, a dreamwanderer;
the fire which is the spirit slaked; the territory which is pain,
scorched.

And then watch out! *Never shit in a shade!*

The flame at the mouth

'In Germany in the Twenties, Harmann, a butcher by trade drained his victims with the twofold practical purpose of selling white meat and black pudding.'

The day that suicide occurs to me I will have to loan an evening suit somewhere so as to be fittingly dressed for the situation. I will wear a dress shirt, with lace stitched to the front, and a bow-tie. — one of those that you have to button on yourself, not the clip-on-kind. My shoes will be black, patent leather and polished, and my socks light yellow. I will have had my hair cut that day for the first time in years, and I will have spattered my whiskers with scent. I will dip in mint water one of those little wooden spoons that you find in ice-cream cups, and then in my mouth on my tongue: it keeps the breath fresh and prevents the tongue from being swallowed. (O, how important the occasion will be!)

I will climb onto a smart chair (my new shoes still creaking slightly) and arrange a velvet chord, a bell-chord, around my neck. Then I will shut my eyes for the last time to see the hills in the darkness, and say: "the dogs hunt for Hannes through the freshly ploughed tomato fields!" and launch myself from the chair into space — I hope I will smile despite the mint-flavoured spoon in my mouth.

After a while the steward will make his call carrying a tray. He will ask: 'did you ring, sir?' and then his thoughts will lose themselves and his eyes will get that far-off look and sunk in his dreams he will spill the glass of liquor over my still slightly quivering socks and shoes. It will be a vodka and tomato-juice, a Bloody Mary, so that it will seem as if I waded in blood. For many years now I have walked ankle-deep in the sickly lurid blood.

'Come and look at the blood in the streets'

blindness can be: an opening out of the inner night
where blood still paces secure and rhythmic
as a sentry on the last level
of a mountain tower
where birds still wear waistcoats
which stretch tighter when the orange-coloured notes
are broken open, still stretched across the silence
like a pure nail in the tree
where the city still stands with a multitude of curtains
rustling as they sweep through all the streets

but death is: everything you lived with
and lived for null-ified
the heart taken from the house the nail on its own —
death means nothing; death is blind and deaf and dumb —
death means that you were never alive
and never absent

and you are dead:
but come and look at the mess in the streets
come and look at the cadavers
come and look at the corpses in the mirrors of blood
and the faces covered with musty newspapers
which don't dare tell the news
which the eyes on their stalks can't read anyway,
        come and look at the dogs scared and plucky — driven by
                hunger, by hunger
which emerge from the grey morning driven by hunger and shy — by
                hunger, by hunger
to howl and tear at what's left
of the socialist dream — yankee and soldier
are the patron saints of the Santiago curs —
come and look at the flies and the dust and the steel —
open your eyes wide, Neruda
                        come and cry over your people

The stars are worms in the universe

a roof over my head
and food in my belly
I thank my stars

a roof over my head
and food in my belly
and wine in the throat
I thank my stars

a roof over my head
and food in my belly
and wine in the throat
and a woman between the legs
and a sun on the mountain
and a bird in the sea
I thank my stars

a roof over my head
and food in my belly
and wine in the throat
a woman between the legs
and a sun on the mountain
and a bird in the sea
and shoes against the mud
and a bum at the door
and wind in the sand
and a god for my prayers
and a devil for my doings
and matches for my pipe
and a morning for my nights
and a death for my life
and worms the length and breadth of my body
o I thank the stars:
thanks, thanks so much, dear stars

Friday 1st February

the nights grow sleek again o my love
like an animal which can boast a new pelt
in the face of winter and the still cold earth
there comes a suppleness a suspicion of warmth
in a couple of buildings lights burn late
an easier laughter slipping across the courtyards
my wife, are we becoming as young as in earlier
poems? I feel my skin and my blood
with delight

I hear the rumble of trucks like snoring birds
from a remote summit arrows are unleashed
I lie within the orbit of your parting-and-returning
breath

you are here and I yearn for you

Gevaar/danger/ingozi*

tauten the tripwires
(call it strophes)
bind the wires with black ribbons
to mark out
an explosive zone
if the whole thing is finely rigged and responsive
then the slightest glance will trigger
a sudden unhatching-of-the-situation
guts, hair, dreams, toe-nails and hatchway
dripping with blood
blasted sky high

*Gevaar/danger/Ingozi: 'gevaar' and 'ingozi' are the Afrikaans and Zulu words, respectively, for danger. This threefold warning is particularly to be found, accompanied by a skull and cross-bones, outside military and technical installations in S.A.

These poems appeared, in chronological order, in the following places:

I'm no travel agent in *Raster No. 2* 1972

Je s'use, The flame at the mouth in *Raster No. 4* 1972

Gevaar/danger/ingozi in *De Vlaamse Gids No. 6* 1974

Friday 1st February, The stars are worms in the universe,
Come and look at the blood in the streets appeared in
the stencils of the *Poetry International Festival*, Rotterdam, 1974

from

Katastrofes

(Catastrophes)

1964

Fascistiese pampoen

'n Man het 'n pampoen gekoop vir sy verjaardag die sestiende september. Hy het die pampoen in 'n ou koerant gevou en dit sorgvuldig onder sy arm gehou. Op pad huis toe het die reisigers in die bus hom agterdogtig aangekyk en die kondukteur het ontevrede vlak agter hom sy snor kom stryk. Hy weet nie of dit sy verbeelding was nie maar dit was kompleet asof daar 'n grommende geluid van die pampoen kom. Tuis het die man die eentonige trappe na sy vyfdeverdieping-woonstel blasend opgeklim en hy had moeite om die deur oop te sluit want hy moes die pampoen al stywer onder sy blad vasklem. Sy swartoogdogtertjie het hom kom soen en gesê naand pappa wat het jy onder jou arm. Sy vrou het stuurs iets gebrom en gevra wat nou so danig in die vuil ou koerant mag wees en gekla dat sy moeg is. Die man het gesê dis 'n pampoen wat ek gekoop het vir my verjaardag die sestiende september en sit dit met sorg in die yskas sodat dit vars kan bly. Sy vrou het gesê dat daar vis sal wees vir aandete en die kind het nuwe skoene nodig vir die skool Skielik was daar 'n kabaal vanuit die yskas en sy vrou het gaan kyk en gegil die verdomde pampoen het die vis opgeëet. Die man het haar probeer gerusstel dis maar net 'n ou pampoen kom laat ons hom op die vensterbank in die aandlug sit om af te koel dis vir my verjaardag die sestiende september. Maar in die môre was die pampoen weg en van die dogtertjie het slegs haar ou skoene onder die bed oorgebly. Die man se vrou het vir dae aaneen geween. Die maan het kleiner geword soms het brokkies daarvan op die aarde geval on toe opeens een aand was daar 'n groot rooi rollende grommende bal soos 'n pampoen in die naglug. Nou het die man geweet sy dogtertjie is die prinses in die maan. Maar hy was diep ongelukkig. Hy het sy kop vasgehou en gekreun my pampoen my pampoen wat sal ek nou hê om aan te smul vir my verjaardag die sestiende september.

Fascist Pumpkin[26]

A man bought a pumpkin for his birthday the sixteenth of September. He wrapped the pumpkin in an old newspaper and tucked it carefully under his arm. On the way home in the bus the passengers looked at him suspiciously and the disgruntled conductor came right up behind him stroking his moustache. He's not sure if it was his imagination but it seemed exactly as if a growling sound came from the pumpkin. Reaching his building, the man puffed his way up the monotonous steps to his flat on the fifth floor and unlocked the door with difficulty having to clutch the pumpkin all the more tightly under his arm. His little blackeyed daughter came to kiss him and said hello dad what have you got under your arm. His wife mumbled something sullenly and asked what on earth could be under the dirty old newspaper and complained that she was tired. The man said it's a pumpkin that I bought for my birthday the sixteenth of September and put it carefully in the fridge to keep it fresh. His wife said there will be fish for dinner and the child needs new school-shoes. Suddenly there was a rumpus from the fridge and his wife went to look and screamed the damned pumpkin has eaten the fish. The man tried to calm her down but it's only an old pumpkin come let's put it on the windowsill in the evening air to cool down it's for my birthday the sixteenth of September. But in the morning the pumpkin was gone and of the little daughter all that remained were her old shoes under the bed. The man's wife mourned for days on end. The moon grew smaller sometimes little bits of it fell to the ground and then suddenly one evening there was a great red rolling grumbling ball like a pumpkin in the sky. Now the man knew that his daughter was the princess in the moon. But he was deeply unhappy. He clasped his head and moaned my pumpkin my pumpkin now what will I have to tuck into on my birthday the sixteenth of September.

The totalitarian pumpkin[27]

A man ordered himself a pumpkin for his birthday the sixteenth of September. Leap-year. He ordered the pumpkin by a smugglers' route it isn't possible to reveal secrets. While he was waiting for the order, he let his fingers click sharpened his teeth gave his tongue moisture and rubbed up his eyes against the lapel of his moleskin jacket until they shone like handcuffs. The man's daughter is an Afrikaans slut out there in the moon. His wife is the other side of the bars the pumpkin will be a sun for him in his sadness for his birthday the sixteenth of September. Leap-year. There is the pumpkin the pumpkin has come where is the pumpkin? The warder has cut the pumpkin open and scooped out pumpkin. The warder has taken out a saw without teeth and three drained dreams wrapped in a manuscript and a pistol full of little hallelujahs and a moustache and a Playboy and a pellet of marijuana and on top of that a future and an escape and three ounces of sympathy from an unknown sympathiser. Then the warder closed up the pumpkin again and said you can't keep a pumpkin in your cell it's against the regulations we are going to put it away until you're released one day (ha ha) away with you little pip where's the evidence now? And the man waited for release or laughter. And the years dragged on and on and the pumpkin shrivelled and shrivelled. Would he receive a little yellow wart in a matchbox on that day and with stiff fish-hooks worn gums and tinted glasses would he find a moon in the little wart and behind the moon a tree and in the tree a little bird and in the little bird a song singing of a wart and in the wart the bones of his past and the blue pips of oblivion. Pumpkin, o my pumpkin! Grab what you can get. Grab the sixteenth of September Leap-year.

envoi-moi mon moi!

It would have been better if the pumpkin had ordered a man for its birthday on any day of any year. And self.

114

Sense of values ho! Mannequins

It's a nasty affair I must confess to my dismay that it's a nasty affair and how to extricate myself now there's a brain-teaser for you because I'm sure I'll soon be living seclusion friends gone even Mr Hiert refuses to water his lawn on Saturday afternoons and it all began so innocently. I bought this rare black little swimmer at the fish market an old lady with purple teeth had him in a sticky jam-jar and my first impression was ha-ha she's trying to palm a pig in a poke off on me because he was lying apparently lifeless at the bottom of the jar but then he moved his little hands and after a polite squabble over the price I bought him for 50 centimes and carried him home I was feeling good and onto the windowsill into the fish-bowl he was plunged a sluggish thing lying basking in the weak winter sun for days on end grew slowly strange oily-black and smooth. And the water turned yellow. Suddenly one day I realised o lord it's plain ordinary urine and peered furiously jaws working over the fish-bowl urine chucked out I was the hell in. When he lay sploshing on slippery bottom suddenly his little fish-bone voice piped up: *Sense of values ho! Mannequins !* I was naturally flustered hands trembling and carefully poured fresh tap water into his glass-house he was contented. And he grew bigger. Fish-bowl too small. Was transferred to basin from basin to bucket from bucket to tub from tub to tank and now lives in the bath in the bathroom and has not changed much except that his voice is stronger and wears glasses and his talent for urinating is disconcerting I spend my days with mopping-up cloths etc. because he also flaps around these days and sometimes even sits in the garden especially now that summer hangs from the trees. The neighbours complain I try my best to calm them down but o lord especially since during the last few days he has taken to pissing through the hedge into someone else's yard Mr Hiert's lawn is down to stubble. And the police have come around grumbling that the sewage system can't dispose of all the urine the whole neighbourhood stinks people are packing up and leaving the neighbours say that they are disturbed at the most impossible moments silence shattered by a booming cry of: *Sense of values ho! Mannequins!* What should I do? It's a nasty affair I must confess to my dismay that it's a nasty affair and how to extricate myself now there's a brain-twister for you because I'm sure I'll soon be living in seclusion friends gone even Mr Hiert refuses to water his lawn on Saturday afternoons and it all began so innocently. But it could have been worse. Now if solids had formed part of his diet.

Yellow peril

'He of this world who allows living creatures, whether once- or twice-born, to suffer, who finds no sympathy within himself for living creatures, let him be looked upon as a pariah' *(Vasalasutta)*

When the night grew deep and thick I woke up with a hiccup the darkness was throttling me I stood up quiet as a mouse so that my wife (wandering in dreams through palatial shops full of coats and shoes, snoring gently with displeasure) would not be disturbed my head shaking walked to the wash-basin switched on the light click white WHAT THE HELL the floor was alive with cockroaches. I was terrified out of my wits. But with hands shading eyes the black shell-bearers scuttled fleet of foot down the unobtrusive little black holes along the skirting-board. When the sun came out I sniggered to myself at my scary-pants fright of the previous night but the next night it was exactly the same. And when we came home in the evening the fat-arses were already sitting there haggling over our daily bread as if a great drought prevailed where they came from. Only the light frightened them away. I was subsequently convinced that by day they would make for a place where it was night. But at the same time they were fast breeders. And they must have decided that I was at a loss. Some of my friends would have liked me to drown or smother them but how could I? Should I make an outcast mongrel of myself? Their little holes in the floor interested me. So one peaceful-steamy day I therefore tried to measure their depth and let one end of a reel of cotton down into a hide-out: after 47 reels of cotton, 8 hours and 24 minutes of unreeling there was a light tug and when I had eventually wound the cotton up a strange oval-shaped rice grain swung from the end. Now that they realized my dilemma they became less modest and one fine morning I'm blessed if there weren't actually about ten of them sitting on the floor yapping away. That was the bitter end. Bending down I noticed that they were wearing dark glasses and heard with a shudder that they were talking Chinese! My house is for sale and I am ready to consider/accept/grab at any reasonable offer. I now work as a deep-sea fisherman in Hammerfest.

Fragment of a quittance

I saw a pumpkin-faced man dipping his dry red beard into a tankard of beer black as a winter's night and refusing to pay and I walked out of the bar revolted and outside I saw a youngster with one wasted hand useless at his breast like a flabby rose he was wearing pink shoes and I walked down the puddle-wet road with the wind in my trouser legs past a tree propping its branches on a curved wall leaning over into the road whistled at the girls and turned in at a blue door ran up the stairs displayed my teeth in a thin smile to a cat and a dog and a baby with a snotty nose and a woman with dirty toe-nails and a man with shoulders bashful as the knees of school-girls and I sat on a chair eating fish with tomato sauce and radishes and peas and potatoes in their skins and butter and bread and lettuce and sweets and belched and laughed and heard the rain like the feet of pigeons on the roof and against the windows and an aeroplane god knows how high in the sky and I looked into the green little humps of the man's eyes and looked away and looked back and I trod on the cat's tail and I stood up and scratched my ear and farted silently in the corner and walked out of the door down the stairs through the blue door and saw that the road was wild and blue as a winter sky and walked in it thinking with compassion of the fate of my poor drenched toes but still and I saw a man hanging onto a lamp-pole and a woman sitting on a pavement peeling potatoes and mountains behind the towers of the cathedrals of a town and a bus tinkling like an old piano and a newspaper wearing a hat on the steps of a block of flats and a bare-footed sparrow sitting smoking in a palm tree and I told my nose and ears of all my sweet secrets.

War and old age

One morning when we got up the war was all around us it was a sunday and the streets were full of semi-clothed men. I have never been a full-time soldier but as always during a war I had a burning desire to be one. Only the professional soldiers were wearing shirts. We of the reserves had to be content with trousers and boots and helmets. Everyone was thoroughly well aware that we could never escape this war that it was only a question of time. I ran to where the town changed to farm-land and was able to see the small green men rushing through the vineyards towards the town here and there our forces stood up to them sniping from behind circular walls. I ran back through the teeming streets the church bells rattling back to camp of full-time soldiers where my brother with the tired eyes was to be found. I wanted him to make me a lieutenant (he himself was one). He conjured an extra shirt up from out of his tent and I put it on but he didn't have any extra insignia then we just painted up a phial to look like a crown and fastened it to my shoulder. And above the left hand pocket of my shirt he wrote in white letters: LIEUTENANT. Then we shook each other's hands and my brother with the tired eyes climbed into his tank and rode out to where the small green men were closing in on the town. But I was frightened and ran in the opposite direction deeper into the town. Past the church my father was standing on the steps with his psalm

118

book in his hand and reprimanded me seriously one should be in
church on sunday what's all this nonsense about war on a day of
rest? But I couldn't obey because I was a soldier and the little green
men were devouring the town from all sides we couldn't escape the
war it was only a question of time. I had to rush on deeper into the
town until I reached a group of slovenly soldiers bundled together
with their arms around each other's naked shoulders in someone's
garden between the vines. Someone had set up a film projector
outside just like that in broad daylight and was now busy showing
an old italian film to the soldiers. Some were crying and others were
laughing shy and self-conscious. But I had to carry on it was only a
question of time. And when it grew dark I went together with many
others to spend the night in the poor house of an old lady. The floor
was covered with bodies like a cornfield full of cobs. Halfway
through the night I was woken up by the noise of animated voices
and went to the kitchen to investigate. The landlady had a visitor a
silverwhite old lady in black garments and a hat and the two old
people were busy drinking coffee and chatting about the price of
sardines it was monday. Everyone was still sleeping it was hardly 3
o'clock in the morning the sun was already lying in splashes broad
as hands on the floor, pouring over the windowsills until the panes
were full. You see LIEUTENANT said the old lady with a cackle,
it's easier for us old people to get up. We're just wasting our time
in bed.

Bloody mess[28]

They wanted to make a monk of me. I remember being shut up with
a handful of other young men in a walled-in forest. It should have
been our paradise but there was too much dust. Still, everyone was
so gentle. They taught us to shoot with a bow and arrow. And in the
evening under the showers I leered scornfully at the pretty plant-like
bodies of the others. Sometimes we had to sit erect for nights on end

119

humming with candles between our interlaced fingers. We lived in tents or hollowed out river banks. But the authorities weren't aware that my wife sometimes clambered over the wall to bring me food and sleep with her legs across my hips. And when I learned from a reliable source that some of the boys had escaped over the wall and gone back to the town I decided that I too would get away. And I bought myself over with the argument that I was no christian anyway. For years I lived outside the wall and sometimes peered over it at the bony half-men who wandered up and down between the trees and down to the sandy walls wearing nothing but sweaters. One day I climbed back over the wall. In the forest I saw a collie dog and a goose on the path each obviously very much in love with the other. When they saw me they blushed but continued proudly on their way. And I went to stand behind a tree with my head between my arms.

Suicide 1

(to Jim)

Was it suicide? And if so, why should it have been? It was once upon a summer's day and the whole land was yellow, the scaly earth boiling under our feet. There was a carnival in the town but we were sick of it, turned around and walked away to this bare knuckly plateau. The blazing white town was far behind us. With lifted eyes he told us that the earth around here was hostile but we wouldn't believe him. We walked further with our eyes on the hot ground and on hearing a cry swung around disconcerted and he was gone, leaving only his volume of poems in the dust. The hollow resonance of his desperate screams rose up to us muffled from the bowels of the earth. O God J's fallen into the ground Arlene began to scan and my wife was also crying bright tears through her nose and my stomach felt empty. I peered through the crack and saw you far below doubled up on your back your arms and legs twitching in the sky

120

like a bellowing bug. Strings of incomprehensible words bellowing up. What could I do? To one side there was the eye of an underground stream which must surely flow past you. I eased my forequarters into the blue hole (spying to begin with) and then pulled my head out, spluttering and my wife asked with wormy hands if it was deep. But I am a brave fellow, took a deep breath and swam off nosing down the pot-hole around a corner and shot up to the surface of the subterranean water like a cork. Climbed out and went to sit on my haunches and talk to you. You smiled broadly with your brown freckled head. You were weak and drunk and white-eyed but there was a chance that we could haul you up by a rope through a split in the earth's hide where the light filtered in and we could see the four anxious eyes of the two women (like phosphorescent eggs in a nest). The patch of blue sky was mysterious as the flaming paintings on a church window. Arlene unwound one end of a coil of mountaineering rope. Laughing, I explained to you how it would be like child's play and scrambled with a wheezing windpipe up the rope through the crack to ground level and peered back encouraging you come on J. You grabbed the rope tightly between rows of fingers and began climbing and sliding but when you were half-way up you cried and let go and fell with a crash into the water. You popped up again once above the swirling blue screamed and disappeared again. For a long time we remained sitting on the ground just as we were. Then I walked to where his book lay in the dust picked it up and opened it. Suddenly a whirring came from the book and the sound of a heavy wingflapper in the sky.

Suicide 2

Was it suicide? Who would know? And if it was, then why was it? But everything, everything is normal when one is a bus driver. I am. In this particular case I had to discharge my load of tourists in a fashionable coastal town. It was already evening an expanse of blue when we rounded the last pass of the mountain range and followed the bending road down to the sea. A tall woman was sitting on the seat just behind me and every now and then she leaned forward and licked the lobe of my ear. In the small rear-view mirror I could see how her husband's face puffed up and reddened. But this is part of a bus driver's routine. I unloaded my people in front of the hotel where we were all going to stay the night, a gigantic place. Black-coated hotel officials were waiting for us a couple of penguins and perhaps because the hotel rooms were identical it came about that we 3 (tall woman husband and I) (only he didn't know it) landed up in the same bedroom. But that's part of a bus driver's routine. And at about the same time as he was lugging their heavy trunks up the stairs, the tall woman and I were already out of the window over the slanted roof off onto a lower roof down the fire-escape through the hotel garden and onto the beach. The night was exquisitely beautiful, lighted by an unearthly blue moon behind the mountains on each mountain peak huddled a white mysterious city domes gleaming in the light and we could hear pleasant dance-music oozing down to us from the cities. One day said the tall woman we'll just be two little black figures in the streets of one of the cities on a mountain peak. Then we went to lie on the warm sand and touched each other's bodies all this is normal when one is a bus driver. And late into the night we walked back to the hotel. Black-coated hotel officials a couple of penguins were waiting for us and told us anxiously that a certain husband had come to make tearful enquiries about his wife and had it seems found a strange man's peaked cap in his room and had come to borrow a spade because he wanted to rise up and chop off the bastard's head and had climbed out of the window over the slanted roof off onto a lower roof down the fire-escape through the hotel garden until he reached the beach. I assured the hotel officials that the man was simple and slipped a tip into the head-waiter's hand and we all had a good giggle about it. Then the tall woman and I climbed up to our room and went to lie down the bed was warm and touched each other's bodies. This is all part of a bus driver's routine. The husband didn't call again. We came across the spade the next morning alongside a freshly turned heap of sand. He had apparently dug a grave there with the intention of planting my severed head in it and had lain there waiting for us. And a turtle creeping up the sand in the early morning had mistaken him for an egg, pushed him into the grave and scratched the sand back. All that remained was a weak kicking under the heap. But we had to carry on and couldn't stop. I took on a new load of people to convey them across the pass in the mountain range to a fashionable river-side town. A short woman in the seat behind me leaned forward every now and again and bit me in the neck. In the small rear-view mirror I noticed how her husband's face puffed up and turned blue. But all this is normal when one is a bus driver.

Cat, hand

The cat was in love with a hand. But then how could it have been otherwise? Ever since he could remember the hand had been there drowsing on his neck or running along his ticklish ribs. He adored the hand the long nails delineated with sweeping strokes the thumb's chapped black face the seductive calluses on the soles of the fingers. And then the hand, despite being shy, welcomed the cat's courtship with delight. In company for example the hand came unobserved to scratch between the cat's ears or chase across his belly until the cat moaned with the bittersweet pangs of love. Only things couldn't carry on like this forever because hand's twin hand boiling with jealousy flared up furiously when the cat sprang onto hand's belly in the heart of the night and the latter stiff with lust wound his legs around cat's thighs. So they decided to elope and one Saturday hand cut himself loose on the shards of a broken bottle — twin hand couldn't prevent it.

As everyone knows all hands are slaves and hand's cruel owner immediately hired a private detective to track down his escaped slave. Unfortunately for him Jan van Tonder the spy was a sensitive guy. Without undue difficulty he followed the trail of blood to the

123

park. He disguised himself as a rose bush and kept watch patiently. And when one morning three days later the sun came running between the trees and benches like a dog that's been shut in for too long, the hand and the cat advanced cautiously from their hiding place. And came to sit hand in hand near a gardenia.[29]

This manifestation of true love deeply impressed Jan van Tonder and when the tears began to trickle down his nose he grew panicky and stuffed a leaf up one nostril and then when he sneezed due to the itch there was a splutter of rose petals and bees. The lovers sprang up terrified and hand crab-walked away on 5 stalky fingers. The poor souls, mused Jan van Tonder and he submitted a report stating that he could find no track or trace of the lovers.

And from that day on he turned to politics. And when one evening in a drunken stupor he went to buy some bread and insisted to the baker's wife that all hands should be emancipated, she thought he was a communist and cheated him out of 3 cents.

Christmas story

It was Christmas Eve. Even the beards of the trees were white. Wind moved across the snow sniffing. A fine wind. The stiff trees shook their frozen arms the snow fell pluff into the snow. The Danube was covered with a skin of ice.

Ours was a small village. 1,800 inhabitants. Everyone was huddled together around the hearth. The small windows were like the yellow eyes of cats in the night. I remember. We tried to snatch up the glow of the flames in the fireplace with our hands. Peered upwards now and then. Listened with tilted heads to the wind sucking and grunting through the chimney (the wind a wolf trying to blow down the little pigs' house). Started when lumps of snow slid off the

124

rooftop and fell like dead doves pluff into the snow. It was Christmas Eve. White. My uncle was busy blowing on his mouthorgan. Silent Night. My little brother's head (he was only 5) was nodding. His head was too heavy for his neck. He had always been a coward my little brother.

And then. Suddenly. The white night was splintered like a glassball o a roaring bawling caterwauling blaring rising up from the lower part of the village the barking of dogs a high pitched whining gunshots like new years' fireworks bangcrashing bedlam. Wind came tugging startled at the window panes. My uncle sprang up. Kicked the chair over. Blew the lamp out. The last I saw of him his eyes were wild and wide all the better to listen with. My brother began crying. My aunt wailed like a cat in pain. Sshhtt. Too late. Rifle butts spattered through the steamgrey windows someone kicked the door open drunk soldiers with creaking boots bloodshot eyes burst inside holding lanterns. (They were wearing thick military coats. And sheepskin caps). Wind blew the smoke down the chimney. Smoke whirled drunk around the room. Curtains fluttered white as terrified small animals. Someone turned the table over. Someone set the curtains alight and flames licked up against the walls. Someone pushed me in the small of my back. My little brother cried for his shoes. They shot my uncle in front of the back door next to the woodshed in the snow (he died in a little heap like the sparrows in the winter). My aunt's hair fell out of her bun. She plodded through the snow like an hysterical witch. Screaming, screaming, screaming. A soldier without trousers dragged her to the nearest lifeless house. I clutched my little brother's hand tightly. He was crying for his shoes. He had always been a coward, my little brother.

We were all in the market place. There was a big fire right in the middle (the snow around it was orange-gold) and there were people in the fire. People were bellowing like cattle. Milling around. Scum at the mouth. People swinging from doorposts with broken necks and limp hands and bulging eyes like those of doves. I think: Solomon sings o your eyes are as the eyes of doves my love. People lying cut up in the snow with stiff hands and buttocks high in the air.

125

Houses burning like bonfires. People running stirring up stumbling through the snow. Like a dance. An infernal dance. The soldiers are hoarse. They hammer white hot spikes through peoples' ears. People die kneeling in the snow staring stupidly ar the heaps of brain in their hands. They bind people tightly together and set them alight. People run like horses of fire (pegasus) over the white snow. I think: Samson lets loose the foxes with firebrands tied to their tails in the white cornfields of the Philistines. They slice off the girls' small breasts and rub coarse salt into the cuts. Girls dig holes in the snow like demented rabbits. They hang people upside-down from verandas and cleave them with bayonets. Halved people hang in rows and the blood drips piff pff paff into the snow. Their mouths are wide as the mouths of idiots. A dance. An infernal dance.

The market-place was too small. We children all had to go to the church. The school was just next-door. The dead children were thrown into the school toilet (The church didn't have toilets). Soldiers chopped holes into the Danube's skin of ice. People were stuffed under the skin of ice. Hundreds. 1,500 people died with helpless hands with futile eyes distorted mouths. Men were castrated. Everyone was finished off men women children (the dogs ran away).

A soldier grabbed us and ran with us to a house with empty eyes. He stuck us under a bed. The room smelled of apples. His eyes were rolling he was crying his beard and eyelashes were scorched his cheeks were black his hands were red. He was a neighbour. He knocked over a chair next to the door. It clattered. He swore. He ran choof chuff away through the snow. I heard children crying in the church. They were striking the children dead with chairs.

And then it grew still. The white wind disappeared. My tongue was stuck to my palate and my eyes were cork. My little brother clutched my dress he pressed his head between my young breasts like budding pomegranates in the early summer he trembled terrified. He had always been a coward my little brother.

I thought of the white bodies of people in the white snow. And the flecks of red all around. White and red. I thought: and she was with child and busy spinning at the window and she pricked her finger with the needle (there was snow outside) and there was a clear drop of blood and then she thought o it will be a daughter with a skin like snow and lips like blood and I will name her snow-white. I thought: tomorrow the bodies will be blue and bloated (I shivered) and the bodies under the ice will be completely water-logged and the fish (they're also water-logged) will eat the bodies and grow fat. All was still. Except that far away (and coming closer) I could hear the wolves coughing and crying (almost in a panic) with excitement as they rushed sniffing with warm wet noses across the snow (and galloping with ears feeling the air). White wolves walking and sniffing across the snow. White. Even the beards of the trees were white (fresh white beards) and when the trees moved their stiff arms (from which grew people) the snow fell pluff into the snow. It was Christmas night.

Christmas story 2 (retribution)

Almost three years later. It is autumn. There is already a crackling coldness in the air. The sky above the church tower is white. Only the bodies of the surrounding hills far in the distance still retain a certain warmth: the red, brown and gold of dying vineyards. The crust of the earth is already hard. Inaccessibly matted. Everyone is here in the market-place. Big and small. Old and young.

Everyone is in black. The church-bell rings and rings. When the old bell shakes his head, he shakes out the sparrows like pepper from a pepper-pot. The sparrows sit with thumping little bodies in the empty trees. They don't know what's going on. They have forgotten. The fingers of the trees are already wasted. Their fingers stick into the white sky. The leaves have already peeled off·from their fingers.

127

The mayor is standing on a small box. He is wearing a black suit (everyone is in black). He is crying. He tells us about three years ago. I can't hear because everyone is crying.

Nine people are standing against the grey church wall. They are guilty. They were soldiers, collaborators. The priest is one of them. He murdered the children in the church. They were discovered, caught. Each of them has a few hundred lives on his hands. How heavily must this be weighing on them? The church wall was once white, now it is grey. A girl is going to shoot them. She lost all her blood-relatives. Almost a hundred of them. And today it is *she* who is the executioner! What an honour.

The crowd of people moves backwards and forwards like a wave. Everyone is here. Everyone is dressed in black. Everyone remembers. The mayor turns around to look at the wall. Everyone looks at the wall. The priest is stripped to the waist but he is wearing a hat. When they surprised him he was in the school toilet (the church hasn't got a toilet). Sometimes, according to the school children, when you're sitting on the bucket, you can hear cries of help! help! coming from deep in the bowels of the earth. Now the priest is naked to the navel. Strange how wrinkled his genitals are. He refuses to take off his hat.

And there is the girl. She takes aim with the pistol in the white air. She is in black. Everyone is in black.

The first shot cracks, like a Newyear's cracker. Someone makes scratch-marks on the grey church wall and coughs. The sparrows jump up in the trees. Look, they are bewildered. The crowd moves backwards and forwards like a wave. I can't see much. The market-place is too small. All the children are here. It's a school holiday. Everyone is in black. Another shot. And another one and another one. She keeps the priest till last.

She shoots the priest's hat off, his hat rolls in the dust. He groans and falls forward. He thinks he is dead. But the girl laughs (she is mad). And she kicks him in the face: *you stupid old idiot* she says,

I only wanted to whet your appetite. Stand up stand up stand up so that I can shoot you dead properly. She shoots him in the stomach. The crowd breaks like a dam wall and floods towards the church. The church is broken down and burnt to rubble. The smoke in the sky is black feathers on the heads of horses in front of a hearse. The people look like ants gnawing at a caterpillar, or ravens around a dead cow. The church-bell rings and rings. The sparrows fall out of the church-bell like pepper from a pepper-pot.

Now everything is over. We all go down to the river. The river is broad and black. The mayor is crying. He stands on a box and leads us in prayer. Everyone is crying. Everyone is in black. The sky is empty and white like the snow of three years ago. With sunset the blood breaks through. Under the water swim fat fish, their stiff greedy eyes turned upwards.

Second aid

Then we were just about crushed. We heard the massive blast and saw the celebrated and much sought after yes, toad-stool cloud high high up flowering at the extremities of the heavens. And down below a hot wind blew through the streets and through our houses and the flowers wilted even though it was winter the world was still and wide with white snow and the paint on our door-posts and window-frames blistered and peeled off in places. We were disillusioned. For minutes afterwards scorched and crisped up shreds and scraps of meat reeking of disaster fell like toads from the shuddering sky plonk onto the snow and paf onto the roofs. Bloody pieces of finger writhing like earth-worms and feathers and hairs and bits of feet and buttocks. The dogs dug crazily for them in the snow. But we were nevertheless unmoved except by the wind which screamed through the streets. Then I heard wet footsteps on the roof and someone or something tapping urgently against the gutter just above the window. This attracted my attention and I dragged the ladder out of the garage leaned it against the kitchen wall and climbed up and standing astride the roof-top was a grasping angel with one bruised wing his forearms and parts of his hips and thighs a morass of blood. Blood from the openings in his body furrowed the roof-tiles with little bright trickles and filtered chirring into the gutters. I was disturbed. It was naturally unhygienic bad-smelling and made scabs and pretty flecks across the back of the roof of my house but I climbed higher and shifted closer he gaped once twice I could see that his mouth was full of blood and from the slit in his chest he gurgled: be quick be quick, god beseeches help.

from

Om te Vlieg

(In Order to Fly)

1971

In order to fly[30]

'Idly I read the legends of King Chou/And set my sights on the map of strange places/In an instant I am flying through the Universe/ How can such a man ever be unhappy!'
(Tao-Yuan-Ming)

Long long ago — on the 15th October 1963 to be precise — there lived an elderly Vietnamese lady by the name of Madame Ngo Sach Vinh. And I'll be damned if she didn't have seven children. Her third daughter but the fourth-born since one of her three brothers is her senior, was/is a lovely woman named Ngo Thi Hoang Lien Yolande Bubi. One and a half years earlier, despite her mother's opposition, she had married a South African, Breyten Breytenbach, also known as Juan Breyten, a name more sophisticated, more mysterious, smacking of Spanish blood because the prosaic is the enemy.

What does this man look like? (I'll leave her appearance to your idle imagination.) His nose is reasonably straight, a natural watershed between right eye and left eye. Under the wings of his nose there stretches a wide moustache, resembling the wing above an airman's shirt pocket. His nostrils are two dark caverns. His mouth is the wind sock below the pilot's emblem, filled with shrivelled little yellow fruits and the red outgrowth of a lung watching over the ruined crop[31]. Around his chin there clings a beard, a chin-strap to prevent his mouth from hanging open too often. All these things are stuck wretchedly to the oblong egg-head. He has no ears. But there are two arms with hands hanging from them like taps and two legs similarly footed. On his head he wears a white hat crawling with silkworms and ants. The ants think he is a tree and the worms think he is a leper. He also wears a white apron with blood-stains all over it. Sometimes he laughs hopp-hopp, hopp-hopp. Now then.

Above mentioned couple were very much in love with each other. She worked herself to the bone keeping the home fires burning. He was a poet/painter, a good for nothing nationalist dreamer, but harmless. And the whole family lived happily, and then again sometimes unhappily, in Paris.

It was naturally against the laws of Nature itself and above all against the current of the Christian Community's moral principles that two people of different skin colour should live together in community and matrimony and wedlock — because he had a rosy skin and was classified 145 284128w as white although there were no whites in his country, apart from the sick. Nevertheless, he would not abandon his wife for any money on earth, depending, that is, on how much he was offered.

He could not bring his bride back to the land of his birth with its warm turf and orange-blossoms and dancing sea and sun, above all for financial reasons; they were exiles and while no one apart from himself could ever be bothered by his fate, the young man felt himself to be oppressed and ill-treated. It's a pity that no one felt him to be a threat to the existing laws and other things of social import. And how deeply he missed his sun. How he longed for his parents. How he would have liked to walk beside the sea with his friends.

And on the stipulated 15th October 1963 the young couple accompanied the old lady to Orly airport just south of Paris from which she was going to leave for Saigon. She had to go to Saigon to put her affairs in order. Her deceased husband had been an advocate and the widow Ngo had inter alia to arrange to sell his practice. At the time, Vietnam was engaged in its umpteenth gruesome blood-soaked war. Bestial communists from an unworldly hell — still not found on any map — were without any reason cruelly engaged in cutting the throats of the soft-hearted (freedom-loving world constables) Americans and their peaceful collaborators.

It is therefore understandable that the young lovers were concerned about the old lady's fate. An accident occurs more swiftly than a thought.

So it came about that they would go and see the old lady off at the airport. No sooner said than done. At the appointed time they watched the old lady proceeding with the others towards the aeroplane. Behind glass (like horseflies against a pantry window) they fervently waved goodbye. Not that they wanted to get her out of the way. It was a hot autumn day with finely veined fish floating drowsily in the sky like clouds in a pond or streaks of cream on blue milk.

Giants resembling bright bombers were standing on the runway scratching in the tar with impatience. Every minute one would draw up and, crying barbarically, leap up nose first into the sky. Then they circled and headed away over the green revolving apeturd[32] until they were simply irritating specks of silver on the retina. So full of chunky power they were, and their line of flight so graceful. And such was the Boeing 707 to which the widow Ngo Sach gave herself up. Over the loudspeakers a female's smoky Hollywood-style voice announced that the passengers and rockets for Tel-Aviv, Teheran, Bangkok, Saigon, Hong-Kong and Tokyo should report directly to gate 51 for immediate embarkation etc. The old widow was naturally already strapped into her seat. Smoking forbidden! Lights flickered, the jet propelled motors hissed and the almighty, reverberating monster began to roll.

On the bus back to Paris Breyten dreamed of sun and beach and rice-fields fertilized at night by crouched farm-workers, groaning all the while, and palm trees. How he envied his mother-in-law. At the St. Michel metro station he kissed his beautiful better half since she had to return to the office and loafed off basking in the autumn sun to their communal lair on the rue du Sommerard. That will be their last parting — unfortunately this fine character who has taken up so few lines, now drops out of our story.

And he dreamed of flight. All around him there was the sweet odour of annual decay. The day glowed like a rust-brown coffin. Things use up so much energy simply retaining their form and proportions and identity that only death offers the possibility of further development. Death is the release of vitality.

At Boulevard St. Germain he turned left, keeping a bitter eye on his shadow on the pavement. To his right in a blue garden in front of the Cluny museum sat two truncated stone lions surveying the pedestrians with infinite scorn. He noticed the wings behind the lions' shoulder blades. These were obviously two Afrikaans lions, most likely prisoners taken in some war long ago. The museum had previously been an abbey and I can imagine how impatiently the lions must have patrolled the wire fence, their wings wavering, while the monks piously threaded their way through prayer after prayer. Later, discouraged, they remained seated absolutely still in a patch of sun. Their wings were clipped and their swords taken away by the holy fathers. Monks are peace-loving. The lions never cried — they were too proud for that. And cell by cell they turned to stone. The cells forgot Africa. They just went on yearning for something they had already forgotton. And that is the worst of all — a yearning devoid of memory. Now during the winter when it grows colder each year, the snowflakes fall from the trees in their bloody jackets to abuse the lions . . . to disfigure their wings. The monks died and were embalmed long ago; the abbot stands in a glass case in the museum muttering his forgiveness, praying for the pagans of Africa. But their yearnings keep the lions going. They have not even reached the hazy fires of purgatory. Take courage, constrained warriors. Every dog gets its day and the wire-haired terrier gets a week-end.

Breyten saw all this through his own eyes, his flesh marbles, when he walked past the museum (or was it a hospital?). Then suddenly he stuck his arms up into the sky like Moses and said: I will fly! And he jumped and shot up like a sheet of paper in a whirlwind through the empty blue sky, up, so that the agitated sky: wind rolled and hissed past his nose, eyes and ears. Up like a dream. He spun higher and higher changing direction with the slightest movement of shoulder or toe-cap. He crowed letters of pleasure. The wind pounding past his open mouth deftly snatched at the ideas. Just as one plucks baked potatoes from the fire. Below his lap revolved the jigsaw puzzle of the massive pink city. He saw the earth bending away in the distance to both sides of him, the mountain ranges with glistening caps and thin tentacles, buckled horizons of sea, rose-coloured coasts, organized blue pastures full of sheep like fleas under trees like grass and much else besides. Up here the sun shone more strongly, his back was as agreeably warm as it used to be in bed on Saturday mornings when he slept late. He forgot everything and everyone — there was now only a single impulse: to reach a hot country. To hell with the Tundras. So he stretched out and swept off in the direction of the Mediterranean sea.

And what does a man in flight look like from below? Let it not be said that Panus[33] writes with less power than Breyten. Like a pale shadow in front of the sun. In the first place, he is not suitably dressed for the flight. He should have elastic bands around his trouser-legs and shirt-sleeves because here comes the wind already blowing up his clothes. He should be wearing goggles, his eyes are crying. The hairs of his body stand upright in the wind. The ants till his body — behind every hair there sits an ant pushing the worm upright. When the wind comes sucking over the dykes every Hollander comes out of his house to keep the saplings standing. You couldn't have taken a decent photo of him. The speed of his flight twists the expressions on his face because his head is now compressed under a wind-pocket. Like the cow trying to jump over the moon. If you could get him into focus in mid-flight, crouching between him and the sun, you would think *there* is the rose *there* is the shining freshflower *there* is the umpteenth angel being kicked out of heaven.

Assuming that the day is wide open and that in the middle of it you manage to keep your objective between you and the sun, you will think you are seeing a glass ball. Because it is transparent in its thinnest parts. That's why I speak of rose. The thinnest parts of the ball. Where the sun filters through the fleshball it shines, rose-coloured. The sky is full of flowers. His hair is swept flat across his head. Like a tree shoot. At night he sweeps low over the orchards to blow out of the trees those people hung up there. Or he drops his bombs on institutions, jails and butcheries.

How long can a man stay in space?

It's difficult to say because he is obviously not dependent on petrol. His fuel, as you know, is blood.

How does he satisfy the normal demands of nature?

Since this book might fall into the hands of youngsters, these questions are not broached here. But why do some trees smell so bad?

Above Italy he suddenly recognized the bright bomber on its way to Tokyo. A plan germinated in his brain and he laughed into his beard. Since he didn't exactly remember much geography he decided to follow the Boeing. By now the throbbing power of the monster no longer overwhelmed him, it even seemed to him somewhat cumbersome. He himself had to fly more slowly so that the aeroplane could keep alongside.

When the brilliant bird began circling a white city he realized that the first leg of the journey had been covered and immediately fell to the ground like a falcon. By the time the giant had come to a quaking standstill outside he was already sitting upright, comfortable and relaxed in the reception hall, looking through the glass wall, it was scorching outside, and waiting. With a smile. Don't hold his vanity and showmanship against him. He contemplated the travellers coming in one by one to stretch their legs before taking off again. Then he caught a glimpse of his mother-in-law and came closer. When Mme. the widow Ngo Sach Vinh saw him, she stopped dead in her tracks her eyes bulging out of their sockets. She grew white as wax, wiped her eyes so as to press them back into her head, then turned around and trotted with shaking buttocks back to her region of safety, her immediate past: the aeroplane. The cold sweat of anxiety dripped, plopping just like sweat into the dust. We were in the holy land.

Breyten called after her, laughing anxiously, but she trotted even faster. Damn it, of course he should have been more tactful, he should have taken account of her superstition and fear of inexplicable phenomena. But what to do now? He wanted to ask her to meet him in Saigon. He wanted to explain to her that he could fly faster and that he would rather dash off to Saigon directly without taking all these detours and then wait for her there because he had neither money nor passport in his pocket and slow flying was exhausting. If only she would put him up for a short holiday of a couple of days since he didn't understand Vietnamese and besides, police surveillance must be unusually stringent with the war going on. He also wanted her, if possible, to get into radio contact with Ngo Thi Hoang Lien Yolande Bubi — his fine wife in Paris — because he could imagine how upset she would be that evening on finding nobody home. Now it wasn't that he wanted to ask his widowed ma-in-law a special favour, as a matter of fact she wouldn't have been inclined to comply since they had never managed to strike it off; she had never forgiven him the seduction of her favourite daughter and he had never come to grips with her intricate character. Perhaps its elemental nature was beyond him. But now what? He was in a mess. Before he could come to a decision the aeroplane was already up in space again, its nose pressing eastward: Teheran persian magic-carpet-city, Bangkok and temples with gold cupolas, Saigon with cannons and soya and opium (and guavas?) and chinamen on bicycles and lepers.

O well, he thought to himself, I've still got lots of time. It's still early and I fly a whole lot better than that tin crate. Perhaps I'll bump into someone who can lend me enough silver for a cable to Bubi. Crazy that I'm so hard up or I'd buy myself an ice-cream it's hot as

139

hell. So went his thoughts as he rambled curiously deeper down the winding little streets full of bearded merchants with bloody towels around their ears. All the men were wearing long robes and looked in astonishment at the wild stranger in his inappropriate clothes, his corduroy jacket, his white sweater, his sludge-white trousers and shoes — the underpants and socks were out of sight. Donkeys creased up and cocked their ears. Fountains glistened in the low blue sun. Lean orange-coloured dogs pissed against the white walls and buried their bones in the bomb-craters and cackling women sold enormous orange-red oranges. Swollen Jaffa oranges. Better than Outspan, he thought, and on top of that, there's the boycott.

But he dared not stay here. Time was saddled. The flat-roofed buildings were already touching each other all over in their purple shadows. So B walked to the nearest open space, a square, and buttoned up his jacket. Make sure that the pipe and tobacco pouch are securely in the pocket, can't survive without smoking, bloody stupid that I didn't leave the key to the flat with Bubi, o well, she'll come up with something. Swelled up again with expectation and pride and wondered once again how it came about that *he* was the one who could now fly. But quickly dispelled these redundant thoughts, shut the eyes tight, stuck the hands into the air up to the elbows and jumped nearly twelve inches high. Dust swirled and caked his shoes. The women in the square between their Jaffa oranges laughed, startled, the dogs barked and pissed anxiously.

He stretched his eyes very wide and jumped frantically five, six times. But when he became aware of the crowd's silent and mocking eyes he turned and rushed down a narrow street with boys monkeying around and jumping behind him: mister chicken's lost his head mister chicken's lost his head.

What had gone wrong this time? He examined his previous actions and precautionary measures from all angles. His eyes burned with the effort. Every now and then he jumped like a goat into the air and flapped his shoulder-blades. He tried several variations. Perhaps my jacket was unfastened, or only had one button unfastened, or two. What was my hair like? Were my arms straight? Or slightly crooked? Were my crooked knees together? Was my hat firmly over my ears? Perhaps I should grow a beard to disguise myself. O national God. Look he even tried his patriotic faith.

And the jumps grew wilder. Perhaps he had slipped up somewhere. Perhaps the intention was wrong. Yes, that's the mistake, I must write off my selfish sun-seeking ideas and fly back to Paris and my faithful little wife. And again and again he tried until his calves throbbed with warmth. But he could not fly. Had he ever flown?

And it was the morning and the evening of the first day. What is my sweetheart doing now? O my love, your temples are like pomegranates, your breasts like those of a dove, you live in the night like a monkey in the mountains, o your nose smells of apples. My beloved is the house of all I do. For a long time my beloved was lost in the intestines of the crab and I was blind, but I can smell my mistress . . . hear her calling me.

The first night he spent crying and shivering and rambling in leaps and bounds from street to street. Towards daybreak — purple in the east, gold in the mouth of the early morning[34] — an orange dog tore his trouser-leg. The dogs are growing cheeky, they are no longer satisfied with the bones that the ants leave behind. He was petrified with fear.

On about the third day the local population drove him from the city with curses and stones. They thought he was the enemy, they thought he attracted the bombers with his small jumps. Does the sun stumble?

On the fifth day the police caught him on the rubbish dumps outside the city — jumpy, limping and stinking in his corduroy jacket and tattered trousers. He was meticulously combing the place for food, poor soul. At first he was happy. He stammered out his disjointed story. They hit him and looked suspiciously through the photos of Foreign Legion deserters in their files. But as he was not wearing his beard they did not recognize him. When he persisted in his assertions of innocence they transferred him, after three days in a cell full of lice-covered drunkards, to an asylum for the mentally ill full of fleas and ants and worms. Not that it was exactly unsuitable. So that he could mess around there.

Somewhere in the background another patient shrieked and shrieked like a cornered cow. Orderlies wearing butchers' hats pushed the patients on trolleys up and down the long corridors. Sometimes just the trolleys. Sometimes it was a race to see which trolley would reach the latrine first. But almost always they found the door locked, because the big boss himself occupied the toilet for almost the whole day. His leprous head was like a scrap of old flesh wrapped in a towel with blood-stains all over it. Now and then he stuck his wrapped-up flesh through the door or window to curse all living things. "Breyten Breytenbach, you bloody idiot, what are you sitting there moaning about? If you're not happy with the hostel you can just shut your trap, fetch your hat and get lost. You've been told to clear out due to your complaints, your filth and other verbage and if you ever dare show your snout here again I will personally shoot you to pips and pieces". This is what even our hero had to endure. But unfortunately the boss did not keep his word. No one knows of his wife's grief and sorrow in Paris. Perhaps in the end she kept only his pipes and paintings as keepsakes. His friends tried to comfort her. Something they had wanted to do, moreover, for a long time. Perhaps he is still somewhere in Tel-Aviv between drivelling old Jews and raving Arabs, each with his own story of how to fly. The skin on his legs is horny, it's a long time since he brushed his teeth.

Now and then he still jumps even though wire netting is stretched over the courtyard. To keep the bombs out. But for the most part he spends his time crying and pleading and shrieking. He also writes disjointed, egoistic (such a lovely word that I can't neglect mentioning it, it makes me think[35] of licking one's self and beak-like lips) poems in a strange language which no respectful soul can understand and which, moreover, will soon have to die out.

A pity. He was rather talented. Before all this he had naturally written that book about me, Panus. He certainly doesn't trim his beard any more, why should he? and so he blends more easily into his surroundings. Each day his crooked nose gets closer to the heat of his mouth. In a strange land friends must stick together. His beautiful wife recovers slowly from the shocking and inexplicable disappearance of her husband. Mme. the widow Ngo Sach Vinh must already be back from Saigon where the Americans perhaps managed to root out the weeds with the help of their poisoned gasses and firebombs. Peace on earth and good will to all men. Time heals all wounds.

I lay my pen down, I stop typing. Rain pursued by wind licks at my face like invisible orange-coloured dogs sticky strips of flapping coiled fly-paper. The story has run out and this is therefore

the end

and by now the sprinter has [36] also gone past

An alternative ending to the narrative ... will come up with something. Swelled up with expectation and pride, stuck his arms into the sky and flew. With what dignity and pride he swam through the blueness! No frontiers hindering his freedom. He was so free that he didn't even have to define his state. He possessed neither love nor hate, was neither white nor black, he was unrestrained. All flies, if we want to get abstruse, are by definition unrestrained. This applies equally to locusts and angels, even those with only one leg. It was like a dream. Night fell pitchjetdarkblack and so without compass or map he drifted unknowingly away from the safe routes.

Towards morning curtains of mist and rain began to fall: and desperate and spiritless he alighted at length on the rump of a sturdy apple-tree, the ground was too frozen, or too muddy. Strange how many bright bones whirred already in the wind. Suddenly a Chinaman loomed up out of the haze wearing a butcher's helmet and snapped: "Food, food!" Or: "An imperialist fowl for breakfast!" Since B had

143

a limited knowledge of this particular dialect, the one influenced by Mongolian, he could not clearly make out what was being shouted. Nevertheless, the Chinaman thereupon drew his bow and shot an arrow vertically through the throat of the dark bundle in the tree. Now if it had only been in the leg it would not have made any difference. I know of an angel who managed to waft just as comfortably minus one leg. It is told that the Chinaman and his pack-mule (or llama) suffered terribly for days afterwards from constipation, due above all to the corduroy. Peace on earth and good will to all men. Time heals all wounds. And the silkworms would not leave him in peace. They sailed closer with laments of lost lovers and stitched his flesh to his bones.

I put my typing aside (Almost) Rain pursued by wind licks at my face like invisible tail-wagging dogs sticky strips flapping wings of fly-paper. Then the story runs out and it is, so ya see,

the end

and by now the sprinter has already gone past.

Poetry

The book *Lotus* consists of nine sections each of which can be considered
s a long poem, broken into smaller poems. These are connected by a numeral
ystem; some of them are sub-titled. Translations have only been made of
ome of the smaller poems which stand to some extent on their own. No
ttempt has been made to reconstitute the original structure of the book.

An allusion to a poem by the Afrikaans poet N. Pvan Wyk Louw (Saint
gnatius prays for his order) in which he declares to the Lord that pain has its
ses.

The title in Afrikaans is 'seisoenegids' — literally, seasons-guide. But 'sei'
ounds like 'sy' — his. And in the middle of the word are 'soene' — kisses:
ence the use of $(kiss)^3$ as in x^3.

Stambos: local name for the Cape town of Stellenbosch: literally, 'stam'
eans both trunk and tribe; 'bos' means forest.

Kafferpruim tree — Harpephyllum caffrum, a wild plum tree

The Afrikaans word hottentotsgot (or hotnotsgot) means praying mantis.
ere the last letter is changed to a d, so that the last part of the word is 'god' —
ference is being made to the fact that the praying mantis is the Bushman
Hottentot) god.

The title is a reference to the song:

ie handvol vere, die handvol vere
ie Bo-veldse volkies dra geleende klere
 jy't verniet gestry
a jy't verniet gestry
olank as die kind in die tjalie lê
an lyk hy net soos jy

iterally:

he handful of feathers, the handful of feathers
he up-land (Cape) people wear borrowed clothes
 you struggled in vain
es you struggled in vain
s long as the child lies in the shawl
e looks just like you

Boland — Eastern Cape

old Thinksomuch: a reference to the Afrikaans idiom: you think so much,
ant a feather and you'd think a chicken would sprout up./

) Iberonimus von Aken — Hieronymus Bosch

1. 'Feather mattresses' is a partial translation of the words 'patrasse van vere'
'patrasse' are a mixture of 'matrasse' (matresses) and 'patryse' (partridges) ...
nd the mixture is made of feathers.

2 Langa and Nyanga are black townships outside Cape Town.

3 These lines are the Swahili equivalent for what follows in the next two
nes

14   Maatla — fire, in Swahili

15   Wellington — a town in the Cape where Breytenbach's parents live and where he was brought up.

16,   These lines are taken from the official English version of the South Africa

17   national anthem, originally written in Afrikaans and quoted here.

18   The title refers to the yacht race between these two places, organized i South Africa.

19   The island-prison off the Cape for black men held as political prisoner

20   Onrus means both 'restless' and is the name of a sea-side town in the Cap

21   rooikrans — acacia cyclops

22   goggling — Breytenbach says that he will "sit/en julle tande tel" literally, that he will "sit and count your teeth", an Afrikaans expressio referring to the amazement of children in adult company.

23   Hottentotsgod — see note 6

24   These poems were smuggled out of prison illegally. This was late discovered by the prison authorities, who used the poems as evidence in th second court case against Breytenbach (see note to 'Totalitarian Pumpkin below).

25   The Taal is the Afrikaans language. The title refers to the struggle i establish Afrikaans as a language in its own right (and with it, Afrikanerdom

Prose

26   'pompoen' (pumpkin) is also colloquial Afrikaans for a fool.

27   This story forms part of a letter sent from prison by Breytenbach to th Afrikaans writer Andre Brink. The letter formed part of the evidence again Breytenbach in a second court case, held while he was already in jail. He wa charged, among other things, with conspiring to escape aided by a priso warder. The story makes reference to 'The fascist pumpkin' which immediatel precedes it in this collection.

28   The Afrikaans title, 'Misoes', literally means 'ruined crop' — but 'blood mess' is closer to the everyday meaning of the word.

29   The Afrikaans word for a gardenia, katjiepiering, literally means 'kitten saucer'.

30   This is an extract from a book of the same name. It forms a section on i own, which is itself entitled 'Om te vlieg' — In order to fly.

31   Misoes again — see note 28.

32   The Afrikaans word for Apeturd (aapdrol) bears a strange resemblance t the word for earthball (aardbol).

33   Panus (penis + anus) is a second identity which Breytenbach takes o in the story.

34   This is a literal translation of an expression: 'die oggendstand het goud i die mond' means 'get up early and you'll get rich'.

35   Breytenbach actually says that the word 'ekkerig' (egoistic) *rhymes* wi two other words of his own concoction: 'bekkerig' (literally, beakish) an 'selflek' (literally, self-lick).

36   Sprinter = spring + winter (the Afrikaans word, winnel = winter + lente the season during which this part of the story takes place.

BREYTEN BREYTENBACH: BIBLIOGRAPHY

Poetry

Die Ysterkoei moet sweet, *(The iron cow must sweat)*, Afrikaans Persboek-handel, Johannesburg, 1964 (Fourth impression 1974).

Die huis van die dowe, *(The house of the deaf)*, Human & Rousseau Uitgewers, Cape Town and Pretoria, 1967 (Third impression 1974).

Kouevuur, *(Gangrene)* — (literally, *Coldfire*), Buren-Uitgewers, Cape Town 1969 (Second impression 1973)

Lotus (written under the pseudonym of Jan Blom — John Bloom. 'Lotus' is the English for one of the names of Breytenbach's Vietnamese wife; a janblom is a lotus eating rain-frog.) Buren-Uitgewers, Cape Town, 1970.

Oorblyfsels. Uit die pelgrim se verse na 'n tydelike, *(Remnants from the pilgrim's verses after* (or towards) *a temporary)*, Buren-Uitgewers, Cape Town, 1970.

Skryt. Om 'n sinkende skip blou te verg, *(Cry/write. To paint a sinking ship blue)*, Meulenhoff Nederland bv, Amsterdam, 1972 (Second impression 1976, with Dutch translations by Adriaan van Dis).

Met ander woorde. Vrugte van die droomvan stilte. (In other words. Fruits of the dreams of stillness), Buren-Uitgewers, Cape Town, 1973.

Voetskrif, *(Footscript)*, (A book published when Breytenbach was already in prison. He has not given his approval to the final ms.) Perskor-Uitgewery, Johannesburg, 1976.

Other poems have appeared in: *Babel, De Populier, De Vlaamse Gids*, the stencils of *Poetry International*, and *Raster*.

Prose

Katastrofes, *(Catastrophes)*, (Short stories), Afrikaanse Persboekhandel, Johannesburg, 1964.

Om te vlieg 'n Opstel in vyf ledemate en 'n Ode. (In order to fly. An essay in five members and an Ode). Buren-Uitgewers, Cape Town, 1971.

'Vulture culture, the alienation of White South Africa' — an article which appeared in *Apartheid*, a collection of writings on South African racism by South Africans, International Publishers, New York, 1971.

'n Seisoen in die paradys, *(A season in paradise)*, (recounting a journey to South Africa in 1973, including poems), Perskor-Uitgewery, Johannesburg, 1976.

147

Collections of poems

Het huis van de dove (Dutch for) *The House of the deaf.* Including the complete contents of *Die ysterkoei moet sweet; Die huis van die dowe; Kouevuur* Meulenhoff Nederland bv, Amsterdam 1976.

Met andere woorden (Dutch for) *In other words.* Including the complete contents of *Lotus; Oorblyfsels; Skryt; Met ander woorde,* and all other poems published up to the end of 1975.

Blomskrif ed. Dr. Ampie Coetzee, Flower writing (The Afrikaans word for 'anthology' is 'bloemlesing' — literally, 'flower reading') Selected poems. Taurus, Johannesburg, 1977.

In translation

De boom achter de maan (Dutch for) *The tree behind the moon.* Short stories translated into Dutch by Adriaan Van Dis and Jan Lonter, Van Gennep, Amsterdam, 1974.

Skryt with Dutch translations by Adriaan Van Dis Meulenhoff Nederland bv, Amsterdam, 1976.

Feu froid Cold fire — poems translated into French by Georges-Marie Lory Christian Bourgois Editeur, Paris, 1976.

Sinking ship blues. Poems translated into English by André P. Brink, Denis Hirson and Ria Leigh-Loohuizen. Oasis Publications, Oakville, Ontario, 1977.